The Refutation of the Christian Principles

SUNY Series in Jewish Philosophy
Kenneth Seeskin, Editor

THE REFUTATION
of
THE CHRISTIAN PRINCIPLES
by
HASDAI CRESCAS

Translated
with an Introduction and Notes

by
Daniel J. Lasker

STATE UNIVERSITY OF NEW YORK PRESS

Published by
State University of New York Press, Albany

For information, address the State University of New York Press,
State University Plaza, Albany, NY 12246

Production by Bernadine Dawes
Marketing by Fran Keneston

Library of Congress Cataloging-in-Publication Data

Crescas, Hasdai, 1340-ca. 1410.
[Biṭul ᶜiḵre ha-Notsrim. English]
The refutation of the Christian principles / Hasdai Crescas;
translated with an introduction and notes by Daniel J. Lasker.
p.   cm. — (SUNY series in Jewish philosophy)
Translation of: Biṭul ᶜiḵre ha-Notsrim.
Includes index.
ISBN 0-7914-0965-1 (alk. paper) : $39.50   — ISBN 0-7914-0966-X
(pbk. : alk. paper) : $12.95
1. Christianity—Controvertial literature—early works to 1800.
2. Philosophy, Jewish—Early works to 1800.   3. Philosophy,
Medieval.   I. Lasker, Daniel J.   II. Title.   III. Series.
BM590.C6813   1992   91-15118
296.3—dc20   CIP

1 2 3 4 5 6 7 8 9 10

To Joseph and Pearl Dworkin

May the generous be blessed.

PROVERBS 22:9

CONTENTS

ACKNOWLEDGMENTS

Many people have helped me in the study of the philosophical aspects of the medieval Jewish-Christian debate. I am particularly grateful for the guidance and advice of my teacher, Prof. Alexander Altmann, and my friend and colleague, Prof. Frank Talmage, may their memories be for a blessing. Their passings have left a great void in my life.

In the preface to my Hebrew edition of Crescas' *Bittul Iqqarei Ha-Nozrim (The Refutation of the Christian Principles)*, I thanked Dr. Warren (Zeev) Harvey, Prof. Menachem Kellner, Dr. Howard T. Kreisel, and Dr. Shaul Regev for their useful suggestions concerning the research of that edition; much of that research is reflected as well in the notes to the translation. Prof. Kellner, Prof. David Berger, and Dr. Vera Basch Moreen were kind enough to review the English translation and offered valuable insights. I would like to acknowledge as well the help and encouragement which I received from Prof. Shlomo Pines, may his memory be for a blessing, in whose class I first read the works of Hasdai Crescas.

I began this translation of *The Refutation of the Christian Principles* while on sabbatical in the Department of Near Eastern Studies, University of Toronto, and I completed it while on sabbatical as a fellow of the Annenberg Research Institute, Philadelphia. Final editorial changes were made while I was a visiting professor at Yeshiva and Princeton Universities. I wish to thank all those institutions for their support as well as my home university, Ben-Gurion University of the Negev.

As usual my family has been a great source of both joy and assistance. My wife, Debbie, reviewed the manuscript and greatly added to the readability of the translation. My children, Shoshana Rahel, Yonah Shmuel, Adina Yael, Dov Eliyahu, and Noam Yerahmiel, have shown various degrees of understanding for my scholarly pursuits, and I wish to thank them for their patience.

This book is dedicated to my in-laws, Joseph and Pearl Dworkin, who have been a constant source of encouragement and support for my scholarly endeavors.

D. J. L.

FORWARD TO THE
ENGLISH TRANSLATION

The year 1391 was the beginning of the end for Spanish Jewry. In that year the Iberian Christian population arose against the Jews, and many were killed in the riots. Ancient Jewish communities were destroyed, and one hundred years later all the Jews were expelled from Spain. Despite the persecution, the murders, and finally the expulsion, the ostensible goal of the Christian leadership was not to harm the Jews but to convert them to Christianity. The Christians tried to influence Jews not only by force but also by preaching. This period was one of intensified missionary campaigns, and, indeed, many Jews were unable to withstand the pressure and converted to Christianity.[1]

The Spanish Jewish leadership did not sit idly by in light of the renewed Christian threat. Its leaders fought as best they could to save their communities. One of the outstanding leaders was Rabbi Hasdai ben Judah Crescas (c. 1340 – c. 1410/11). Crescas, whose only son was killed in the riots of 1391, was chief rabbi of Saragossa and influential in the court of Aragon.[2]

Crescas is known mainly for his book of philosophy *Light of the Lord*, which was the last major medieval Jewish philosophical work. Crescas' philosophy is characterized by a rejection of the Aristotelian philosophy which had been adopted by his important predecessors, Maimonides (Moses ben Maimon, 1135 or 1138 – 1204) and Gersonides (Levi benGershom, 1288 –

1

1344). One notes in Crescas' philosophical work both originality of thought and brevity of language.[3]

In addition to the Hebrew *Light of the Lord*, Hasdai Crescas wrote two anti-Christian polemics in the vernacular.[4] One book consisted of exegetical arguments based on Biblical verses,[5] the most common genre of anti-Christian polemic. Because of the existence of so many works of this type, no one bothered to translate it into Hebrew, and it did not survive.[6] The second polemical work consisted of philosophical arguments against the principal beliefs of Christianity. According to Crescas, these principles are (1) original sin; (2) redemption from original sin; (3) trinity; (4) incarnation; (5) virgin birth; (6) transubstantiation; (7) baptism; (8) the coming of the messiah; (9) a new Torah; and (10) demons.[7]

The original of this book did not survive, but a Hebrew translation (or paraphrase), with commentary, was written by Joseph ben Shem Tov (c. 1400 – 1460).[8] This book is known as *The Refutation of the Christian Principles (Bittul Iqqarei Ha-Noẓrim)*, and an English translation of the Hebrew version is presented here.

THE ORIGINAL LANGUAGE OF THE BOOK

Joseph ben Shem Tov wrote a number of times that Hasdai Crescas composed his books in the vernacular ("the language of his country"— *leshon arẓo*),[9] apparently distinguishing that language from the language of Joseph's country, Castile. Saragossa was the capital of Aragon, and it is possible that Crescas wrote his polemics in Aragonese. Still, the literary language of Aragon in that period was Catalan, and it is, therefore, reasonable to assume that he wrote in that language.[10] It is impossible to derive any information about the original language of this work from the few non-Hebrew words scattered through it (which are generally corrupt in the manuscripts in any event). The language in which his refutations of Christianity were written remains, therefore, in doubt until the originals are found.

THE NAME OF THE BOOK

Just as we do not know the original language of Crescas' polemical works, we also do not know their names. The extant polemic, against Christian doctrines, has often been cited as the *Tratado*,[11] apparently without basis. J. de Rossi, in his book concerning Jewish anti-Christian polemics, called the work in Latin *Tractatus de articulis religionis*.[12]

The name of the work in Hebrew is also doubtful. The first author to cite this work in Joseph ben Shem Tov's translation, Don Isaac Abravanel, called it "a treatise which he wrote in the vernacular concerning the doubts pertaining to the belief of the Christian nation."[13] Scholars who wrote about Crescas' polemic before 1860 (apparently the year of the first edition) did not know what to call it. Moritz Steinschneider, for example, thought that perhaps the title of the work was *"Ma'amar Ha-Nivdal."*[14] J. de Rossi wrote the name as *Maamar*.[15] In some manuscripts, the title is recorded as *Book of [Your Commandments] Make Me Wiser Than My Enemies*, on the basis of the verse from Psalms (119:98) with which Joseph ben Shem Tov's Introduction begins. In fact, the name *The Refutation of the Christian Priniciples (Bittul Iqqarei Ha-Noẓrim)* is found in only two manuscripts, both from the same scribe, and there it is followed by the words "of Rabbi Joseph Ibn Shem Tov [*sic*], of Blessed Memory".[16] When the first edition was published, the anonymous editor copied one of these two manuscripts and, therefore, he used the title *The Refutation of the Christian Principles*. He added that the book "raises objections to each of the principles of the Christians, called *articulos*." The second edition copied from the first edition. On the basis of these two editions, the name *The Refutation of the Christian Principles* became accepted as the title of

Crescas' work. Nonetheless, it is clear that if the first editor had used a different manuscript, the name *The Refutation of the Christian Principles* would not have become accepted as the title of Crescas' treatise. There are no other references to this title in any of the literature before the first edition, and there is no reason to assume that this is the title given to the work either by Crescas or by Joseph ben Shem Tov. Today, however, *The Refutation of the Christian Principles* is considered by everyone to be the name of the book, and we shall use that title here.

THE DATE OF *THE REFUTATION OF THE CHRISTIAN PRINCIPLES*

In Chapter 8, "Concerning the Coming of the Messiah," Crescas wrote that contemporary Christians needed prophets to lead them because "they have had two leaders as Popes for approximately twenty years. Each one and his followers think the other is excommunicated and punished by Heaven." Since the schism in the Catholic church began in 1378, the natural inference is that this book was written around 1398. Joseph ben Shem Tov's estimation (in Chapter 3) that *The Refutation* was written after the composition of *Light of the Lord*, which Crescas completed in 1410, is, therefore, not reasonable.[17]

CRESCAS' METHODOLOGY

Joseph ben Shem Tov, the translator of *The Refutation of the Christian Principles*, described Crescas' methodology as follows: "The fifth way [of the six ways of anti-Christian polemic] is the method of one who intended to raise objections against each of the principles of belief, called roots '*articulos*.' He thought it proper first to set forth the premises which are admitted by both parties, and those about which they disagree. These polemical treatises lead to either positive or negative conclusions. This is the way of the sage, Rabbi

Hasdai Crescas, of blessed memory, in a treatise which he composed in the vernacular concerning this. It is a very valuable treatise; may God, may He be exalted, reward him for it."[18] This methodology fits in well with Crescas' literary endeavors, since one of the characteristics of his style is the clear formulation of the relevant questions and the thorough analysis of all the aspects involved. In the present work, Crescas recorded the premises on which the Christian principles are based and indicated which of these premises were accepted by both sides of the debate, and which premises were accepted by the Christians alone. His goal was to demonstrate that the premises rejected by Judaism contradicted the premises which were common to both sides. For instance, Crescas argued that it is logically impossible for the Christians to maintain, on the one hand, the premises that God has necessary existence, that He is eternally perfect, that He is simple and noncomposed, and other such beliefs which were acceptable to both Jews and Christians, and, on the other hand, to believe in the trinity, a belief held only by the Christians.

For the sake of the argument, Crescas was prepared occasionally to accept some of the Christian assumptions which he had already rejected. Hence, we read expressions such as: "Even if we should posit the above premise, for the sake of argument, even though it is not true"; "Even if we posit that it is possible"; "Even if it is posited as possible"; "Even if we posit that the trinity is possible"; "Even if these principles are posited."[19] Crescas' intention was to show that the Christian principles discussed in his book are absolutely invalid.

What is the nature of this invalidity? The essence of Crescas' criticism of Christianity is based on two premises which, he asserted, were common to both Judaism and to Christianity, namely, "faith will not force the intellect to believe something which leads to contradiction" and "one cannot imagine that the divine power is able to contradict either the first intelligibles or the derivative principles which have been clearly and absolutely demonstrated, since they derive from the first intelligibles."[20] In other words, religions may not maintain that divine power can guarantee the veracity of absurd doctrines which contradict reason. God is not omnipotent in the sense that He can do the impossible. The purpose of the intellect in religious disputes is to distinguish between a possibly true divine religion and an obviously false religion. A true religion does not teach irrational beliefs. Intellect cannot prove that a divine religion is, indeed, true, because there are theological matters that are beyond the realm of the intellect; nevertheless, the intellect can establish that a particular religion is not divine if its beliefs contradict reason. Crescas' position reflects well the ideology of the Jewish philosophical polemicists who wrote in the fourteenth and fifteenth centuries in Spain under the influence of Averroism (a philosophical school which developed certain ideas of Abu Walid Ibn Rushd [Averroes], 1126 – 1198). Another representative of this school of thought was Profiat Duran.[21]

THE RELATION BETWEEN HASDAI CRESCAS AND PROFIAT DURAN

Profiat Duran (Isaac ben Moses Halevi, "Ha-Efodi," exact dates unknown), a member of Crescas' inner circle, also wrote two anti-Christian polemical works: *Epistle Be Not Like Your Fathers (Iggeret Al Tehi Ka-'Avotekha*, 1394 or 1395) and *The Book of the Disgrace of the Gentiles (Sefer Kelimmat Ha-Goyim*, 1397).[22] According to Duran, the latter work was written to fulfill a request made by Crescas himself. Hence, it may be reasonable that "this composition was apparently intended to serve as the raw material for the polemical work which Crescas himself intended to write, namely *The Refutation of the Christian Principles*."[23] Nevertheless, it is hard to see that there was any real influence of *The Disgrace of the*

Gentiles on *The Refutation of the Christian Principles*. Even though there are some common subjects, such as trinity, original sin, the eternity of the Torah, virgin birth and transubstantiation, Duran dealt with these topics through criticism of the New Testament and not through philosophical analysis. In addition, according to Duran, Crescas himself knew very well how to answer the Christians: "You, the glory of the rabbis, are quite capable of refuting them in these matters . . . and you, the glory of the rabbis, will strike with the venom of your tongue and the breath of your holy mouth, smiting the wicked with the spirit of understanding lips."[24] Hence, there is no real reason to assume that Crescas used Duran's book extensively. It is possible, nevertheless, that *The Disgrace of the Gentiles* was intended as raw material not for *The Refutation of the Christian Principles* but for the second polemical work which Crescas wrote. Yet, this work, according to the testimony of Joseph ben Shem Tov, included proofs from the prophets and was not based on the New Testament. It is also possible that Crescas invited Duran to compose *The Disgrace of the Gentiles* for his polemical enterprise but the book did not meet his needs.[25]

There is, however, a certain affinity between *The Refutation of the Christian Principles* and another book of Duran's, namely *Epistle Be not Like Your Fathers*. Both the presuppositions of the argumentation, namely, that the sciences and logic negate Christianity, and the contents of the arguments themselves, especially against transubstantiation, are similar in the two compositions. Nevertheless, even though *Epistle* and *The Disgrace* were written before *The Refutation*, for the two authors the influence was not necessarily one-sided. Apparently, anti-Christian polemics was one of the important issues discussed in Crescas' circle, and the members of that circle must have exchanged polemical arguments among themselves. Thus, for instance, Duran mentioned in *The Disgrace* that, according to the Christian opinion, the patriarch Abraham's circumcision saved him from Hell.[26] This idea is repeated a number of times both in *The Refutation* and in *Light of the Lord*.[27] It might be possible, therefore, to assume that Crescas was influenced in this point by Duran's work. As a matter of fact, though, the very same idea is already found in the book *Arbaʿah Turim* of Crescas' pupil, Rabbi Abraham ben Judah, which most likely reflects Crescas' own opinions. This book was written in 1378, before *The Disgrace*.[28] It is very probable, therefore, that Crescas also influenced Duran. It is clear that Duran had much wider knowledge of Christianity and Christian literature than Crescas. He was also willing to cite Christian compositions explicitly, something which Crescas did not do. In addition, it is possible that Crescas learned about Christianity from Duran in the course of their private discussions, and not necessarily from the latter's literary works.

FOR WHOM WAS THE BOOK WRITTEN?

Hasdai Crescas started his polemic with the words "Princes and nobles pleaded with me to compose a treatise in which I would present the doubts and refutations which the followers of the Torah of Moses, peace be upon him, can offer against the Christian belief. . . . Since this goal is worthwhile in and of itself, and since I had to fulfill their desire (even though I am unworthy), I saw fit in this treatise to prepare and carefully compose that which they commanded me."[29] Who were those princes and nobles whose desire Crescas felt he had to fulfill?

Heinrich Graetz was the first to assume that Crescas referred here to Christian princes and nobles who wanted to know why Jews refused to convert. Crescas was both the chief rabbi of Saragossa and an important courtier in the court of Aragon. Hence, according to Graetz, the book was intended for the Christian nobility, whose request Crescas could not deny. The writing of *The Refutation* in the vernacular reinforced Graetz's opinion that the work was intended for a non-Jewish audience.[30]

Ben-Zion Netanyahu rejected this conclusion, arguing that there is no reason why Christian nobles would search for the reasons why Jews refused to convert. In his opinion, the "nobles and princes" were Jews who were upset by the mass conversions. Crescas was asked by the Jewish nobility to write a book intended for the recent converts to Christianity for whom Hebrew reading was already too much of an effort (and, therefore, he wrote in the vernacular). They asked Crescas to explain to the apostates why Christianity was a false religion. It is noteworthy that Netanyahu's conclusion conforms well with his theory that the Jewish Conversos christianized of their own free will and did not live secretly as Jews. It was the Inquisition which returned them to Judaism.[31]

In order to decide the issue of the intended readership, it is necessary to point out two facts. First of all, the prospective audience of *The Refutation* was a very learned one. Crescas assumed that his readers both knew and accepted Aristotelian philosophy. As the modern reader will see, this book is certainly not easy reading, and its arguments are often quite complex. The intended reader obviously had a very wide and varied educational background.[32] Second, *The Refutation* is not Crescas' only polemical work. As already noted, he wrote another treatise "in the vernacular," one which responded to Christianity on the basis of prophetical proof-texts. It is hard to imagine that the Christian nobility requested not one polemical book but two.

It follows, therefore, that Crescas' polemical works were not written as an academic exercise but as a means of convincing the readers. Hence, it is reasonable to assume that they were intended for Jews who either were about to convert or had already converted. Many of these Jews (or converts) must have been people learned in philosophy (otherwise, there would have been no place for the type of arguments included in *The Refutation*), who could no longer read Hebrew literature (otherwise, there would have been no reason to write in the vernacular).[33] The fact that there was such a potential readership of Jews/converts shows that there was a great amount of assimilation among the highly educated stratum of Jewish society. Fifty years later, Joseph ben Shem Tov thought it appropriate to translate *The Refutation* into Hebrew because his students could not read works written in the vernacular. This indicates that those who assimilated linguistically eventually assimilated religiously as well. Those who remained loyal to Judaism and wanted the wherewithal to polemicize against the Christians were unable to read books "except in our holy language." There was no longer an audience for anti-Christian polemics written in the vernacular, and Crescas' original compositions did not survive, except for one which survived only in translation.[34]

JOSEPH BEN SHEM TOV'S HEBREW TRANSLATION

In the middle of Chapter 3, Joseph ben Shem Tov noted: "This is how the words of the Rabbi, of blessed memory, should be understood in this place. I expanded the explanation in my translation since his language is brief and recondite in this place, and I have seen no one who could understand it. Hence, I transgressed the rules of translation here more than in the other chapters." We learn, therefore, that it was not easy to translate Crescas' work; that Joseph tried to be faithful to the contents, even if not to the exact wording of the source; that Joseph was aware that there are "rules of translation." Hence, we can justifiably assume that the work as we have it today more or less reflects the original, but it is not a literal word-for-word translation, as were most medieval translated texts. After all, Joseph's aim was to present his students with a "double-edge sword" with which to wage "an obligatory war" against Christianity.[35] For this purpose, there was no need for a literal translation. In addition, Joseph testified in his introduction that this was his second attempt at a translation; the first translation, a literal one, did not fulfill its purpose as a source for Jewish disputants. The new translation would aim at "translating the content of this treatise, not merely translating its language. I will try with all my might to preserve its intention, clearly explaining its secrets and hints, expanding the discussion in each principle so that [the treatise's] benefits spread to all its environs." Joseph ben Shem Tov thought it appropriate in addition to add his own explanatory comments and polemical arguments.[36] Joseph's translation, then, was intended to be easy to read and practical for the disputant.

There are quite a number of signs that Joseph did not execute his translation with a high degree of accuracy. First, the translation was completed in ten days ("the last ten days of Av, 5211," namely August 1451).[37] Second, in a number of places the numbering of the arguments appears to be defective.[38] Third, Joseph wrote at the end of the book, "Here is completed what I have seen proper to translate from these chapters,"[39] implying thereby that perhaps he did not translate the entire treatise. Fourth, it is not always clear where Crescas' words end and Joseph's words begin.[40]

It would be wise, therefore, to be cautious when reading this book. On the one hand, there is no reason to adopt an absolutely skeptical approach which rejects almost any relation between Crescas and *The Refutation* in its translation by Joseph ben Shem Tov. On the other hand, it is proper not to exaggerate any conclusions which might be drawn from this work pertaining to Crescas' philosophical or theological positions. Without doubt, the great majority of this book as we have it now was written by Hasdai Crescas. We just do not know with certainty whether we have the entire book or whether everything which appears to us to have been written by Crescas is indeed his. Hence, when dealing with Crescas' polemical enterprise, we must take into account the nature of the work as we now have it. One of the interesting topics of that enterprise is the contradictions between *The Refutation of the Christian Principles* and *Light of the Lord*, Crescas' philosophical work.

CONTRADICTIONS BETWEEN *THE REFUTATION OF THE CHRISTIAN PRINCIPLES* AND *LIGHT OF THE LORD*

The first to note possible contradictions between the philosophical work and the polemical one were people whom Joseph ben Shem Tov called "some scholars" (*qeẓat maskilim*). These people had used Crescas' arguments against the trinity in *The Refutation* in order to refute his own theory of positive divine attributes in *Light of the Lord*. According to Joseph ben Shem Tov, these scholars did not understand that there is a difference between an essential, positive attribute and a person of the trinity. The source of their error was the fact that the word "attribute" (*to'ar*) was often used in place of "person" to stand for the Father, Son, or Holy Spirit. Hence, Joseph suggested, one should translate the word "persona" into Hebrew as "*parẓof*" not "*to'ar*". In reality, according to Joseph, there is no contradiction between Crescas' arguments against the trinity and his theory of attributes.[41]

The case of Crescas' arguments against eternal generation of the Son and the procession (emanation) of the Spirit is different. In this subject, Crescas employed the proofs of Abu Hamid al-Ghazali (1058 – 1111) and Gersonides against the eternal creation of the world in order to argue that eternal generation and emanation are impossible. Joseph ben Shem Tov correctly noted that Crescas himself not only believed in the eternal emanation of the world but also tried (without success, according to Joseph) to refute those very same arguments which he used in *The Refutation*.[42]

Joseph ben Shem Tov could have added a number of other contradictions. In *Light of the Lord*, Crescas argued that eternal life was achieved by means of observance of the commandments, not by intellectual achievement; in *The Refutation*, Crescas wrote: "We maintain that he who worships God can achieve [this reward] naturally by means of his speculative life which causes pleasure to his holy soul, so that he inherits eternal life. It is proper to maintain this position."[43] In *Light of the Lord*, Crescas adopted the belief in original sin; in *The Refutation*, he rejected this belief.[44] In *Light of the Lord*, Crescas polemicized against Aristotle's definition of time; in *The Refutation*, he used it against the Christians three times.[45]

Before dealing with these contradictions, it is important to pay attention also to those aspects which are common to the two works. For instance, the justification of the eternity of the Torah in *The Refutation*, Chapter 9, has quite a number of similarities with *Light of the Lord*. Three special miracles, namely, the defense of the property of pilgrims, the good harvest in the year before a Sabbatical year, and the efficacy of the waters of a woman suspected of adultery (*mei sotah*), show that the Torah is true. From the stories of Enoch and Elijah, and from the blessing of Balaam, it is possible to understand that the Torah teaches that there is eternal life. The Torah was given to a people on a high intellectual level, a nation that did not assimilate in Egypt.[46] In addition, Crescas' method of argumentation, his brevity of language, and certain linguistic forms are evidence of the relation between the two compositions.[47]

The question which can be asked, therefore, is how one can explain the contradictions between the two books. Joseph ben Shem Tov, the translator, suggested that *The Refutation* represents a more advanced stage in Crescas' thought.

After having written *Light of the Lord*, Crescas changed his mind about the possibility of eternal creation and, therefore, used Gersonides' arguments, which he had rejected in his philosophical work. This opinion is not reasonable, since Crescas wrote *The Refutation* approximately in 1398, whereas he finished *Light of the Lord* only in 1410.[48]

Shalom Rosenberg has also proposed a developmental theory to explain the contradictions between *The Refutation* and *Light of the Lord*. According to Rosenberg, Abraham ben Judah's book *Arba'ah Turim* represents the early stage in Crescas' thought even though it was written by his student. In contrast, *The Refutation* reflects Crescas' developing thought, and *Light of the Lord* is a product of his later thought. Rosenberg believes that Crescas' views concerning physical and metaphysical questions developed while those dealing with theological and religious questions remained constant. *The Refutation* is, therefore, an intermediary stage between *Arba'ah Turim* and *Light of the Lord*.[49] It appears, however, that it is difficult to make such a clear distinction between various periods in Crescas' development. For instance, in *Arba'ah Turim* and in *Light of the Lord*, there is a belief in original sin; in *The Refutation*, Crescas rejected this belief. In any event, it is impossible to agree with Rosenberg's opinion that there is "an extreme affinity"[50] between *Light of the Lord* and *The Refutation* concerning theological matters.

Without establishing definitely the relationship between *The Refutation* and *Light of the Lord*, it would appear that one should be cautious not to conclude too much from the polemical work. Crescas' goal here is to provide answers to Christian arguments. Since his opponents believed in original sin, Crescas rejected this belief. Since they accepted Aristotle's definition of time, and this definition contradicts other Christian beliefs, then Crescas was willing to adopt that definition. Christians believed in eternal generation of the Son and eternal procession of the Spirit; Gersonides' arguments against eternal creation seemed to Crescas to be useful in combatting these doctrines, and, hence, Crescas used them. Polemics, like love and war, has its own rules.[51]

THIS TRANSLATION

The present English translation, the first in a modern Western language, is based on my edition of Joseph ben Shem Tov's Hebrew translation of Crescas' polemic.[52] I have attempted to be faithful to the Hebrew text, aiming for both literalness and clarity. I have also tried to achieve consistency by regularly translating Hebrew terms with the same English terms to the extent that the content justified such translations. Words or phrases which are not in the Hebrew but are necessary for an understanding of the text were added in square brackets. Arguments have been numbered or lettered for easier comprehension. Scriptural quotations are generally cited according to the Revised Standard Version, unless content required otherwise. I have distinguished between Crescas' original (as represented by Joseph ben Shem Tov) and Joseph's own interspersed comments and notes by using two different fonts. All emphases have been added to the text.

In my notes to the text, I have referred to parallel Jewish and Christian sources. The citing of a particular Christian text should not be taken as an indication that I believe Crescas actually used that text but only as evidence to support his claims concerning Christian beliefs. Thus, I refer to Thomas Aquinas often because his works are readily available. Unlike Duran, Crescas did not explicitly mention his Christian sources.[53]

THE REFUTATION
of
THE CHRISTIAN PRINCIPLES

Joseph ben Shem Tov's Introduction

YOUR COMMANDMENTS MAKE ME WISER THAN
MY ENEMIES; FOR IT IS EVER WITH ME[1]

[I shall begin] after praise and glory to the infinite God who, from His essence, has apportioned for us that equity and felicity through which we can become perfect and happy. He has guarded us from perplexity and confusion and has taken us from among the nations to be a people of His own possession,[2] a kingdom of priests and a holy nation,[3] servants of the Most High. [We are] those who reflect the truth, expert in war,[4] and separated from blunders, for God has separated us from those who go astray[5] in order to bask in the emanation of His glory. He has not designed our destiny to be like theirs, nor our lot like that of all their multitude.[6] All of them act shamefully and disgracefully[7] because of their doctrines and beliefs. They are like an animal in the shape of man, separated from the sensible, isolated from the intelligible.[8] The father teaches lies and deception to the children.[9] They bow down to vanity and emptiness and pray to a god that cannot save.[10] But we, His people, the sheep of His pasture,[11] bow before the King,[12] the Lord above all nations, mighty to save.[13] He shined upon them the Torah of truth from the place He made His abode.[14] His throne is in the heights of the world — a divine throne[15]— and the justice of his righteousness reaches to the ends of the earth. Yours, O Lord, is the greatness and the power.[16] You are blessed and exalted above all blessing and praise![17]

I beheld the rigor of exile, the exile of Jerusalem in Sepharad,[18] with enemies' devouring us and crushing us every day,[19] enemies who intend to destroy us,[20] boasting,[21] saying to me the whole day: "Our fathers inherited naught but lies";[22] my heart was filled[23] with a willing spirit,[24] and I commented upon an important epistle dealing with the principles of their belief

19

according to rational demonstration. Its foundation uproots their principles, saying: "Raze it, raze it! Down to its foundations."[25] This is the well-known *Epistle* of En Profiat.[26] At the beginning of my commentary, I mentioned six ways in which our righteous predecessors polemicized against the spokesmen of this nation.[27] In the fifth one, I mentioned what was done by Rabbi Hasdai, of blessed memory, in a treatise, small in quantity but great in quality and eminence,[28] which he composed in the vernacular.[29] Because of its brevity and depth, its benefit has escaped the members of our nation. In addition, its language is strange for those who have not been accustomed to study science except in our holy language, and, therefore, its contents have remained like the words of a book that is sealed.[30]

As I have been tranquil and peaceful, guarding my house of study, His lamp shining upon my head,[31] my students surrounding me, I translated it for them into our language in order to show the power of His works to the nation of God, His heritage.[32] Since, however, believers have been removed and men of science have been lost,[33] only those who do not know the law of the God of the land have been left.[34] They were not able to derive from it the secrets of existence and the divine mysteries, because of the brevity of his language and his excessive use of indirect allusion, both in what he noted and in what he omitted. Most of those in our generation who engage in speculation[35] cannot understand his intentions, may his memory be for a blessing. The most worthy of its benefits have been lost to them, for there is no one who is understanding and wise in this land[36] who can understand him without a true guide.[37] And so, because of my love of truth — the Lord is the true God![38]— and my desire to cause sons — sons of the living God[39]— to ascertain the truth; and to put in their hand a double-edged sword[40] in order to arise in war — an obligatory war — to give a true answer[41] to the pursuer; to give instruction in the foundations [of the truth] to youths without blemish, endowed with knowledge, understanding learning, and competent to stand[42] in the breach, who have requested that I return to the labor of translation, [this time] not merely to transpose the language but to translate its contents,[43] and to add a complementary commentary in such a perfect manner so that its benefit and desirable fruit be publicized, so that his teachings live unforgotten in their mouths;[44] I have acceded to their request.[45]

I hope that God, may He be blessed, will reward me, a fugitive and a wanderer in the land[46] of my affliction, by allowing me to behold His majestic glory soon, as He removes abominations from the heart of men,[47] as all flesh shall come to worship before Him,[48] accepting the yoke of the kingdom of heaven, which He gave at Sinai, for the earth shall be full of the knowledge of the Lord.[49] I begin to do this with the help of God, translating the *content* of this treatise, not merely translating its *language*. I will try with all my might to preserve its intention, clearly explaining its secrets and hints, expanding the discussion of each principle so that [the treatise's] benefits spread to all its environs.[50] He[51] said:

Ḥasdai Crescas' Preface

Princes and nobles[1] pleaded with me to compose a treatise in which I would present the doubts and refutations which the followers of the Torah of Moses, peace be upon him, can offer against the Christian belief; and that, by evaluating the positions of each side, I should intend by means [of composing this treatise] the worship of the Creator, may He be blessed, by establishing the truth in the ancient dispute between the Christians and the Hebrews. Since this goal is worthwhile in and of itself, and since I had to fulfill their desire (even though I am unworthy), I saw fit in this treatise to prepare and carefully compose that which they commanded me.

So that the truth may be seen in the clearest manner, by eliminating all deception or equivocation, I saw fit to prefix two statements.

1. Since one cannot avoid using some premises in order to attack or to defend, it is proper that the premises which are common to the two parties, namely, those to which the two disputants give assent, should be readily available.

2. Given that the intention of this treatise is to set forth the doubts and the refutations which follow from the Christian belief, it is proper to set forth the intention of their principles and to conceive their true meaning, since the concept of something precedes its verification.[2]

23

Since the setting forth of the premises, both those which are common to the parties and those about which they differ, should be done in regard to every principle concerning which there is a quarrel and fight,[3] I say: There are ten principles of the Christian belief:[4]

1. The original universal sin of Adam
2. Redemption from this sin
3. Trinity
4. Incarnation
5. Virgin birth
6. Transubstantiation[5]
7. Baptism
8. Messiah
9. A new Torah
10. Demons

It remains now to set forth in respect to each of these ten principles the premises which are common to the two parties and those about which they disagree.

First, concerning the first principle: the punishment of Adam.[6] There are three common premises: (1) the punishment was just; (2) the punishment was corporeal and spiritual;[7] (3) the corporeal punishment was not removed and is still in force.[8] There is disagreement concerning one premise: the Christians believe and maintain that the spiritual punishment was the withholding of the grace of paradise[9] from all souls who come after Adam.[10] The Jew maintains and believes that the spiritual punishment pertains solely to the soul of Adam and the punishment did not pass on to any other soul.[11]

Concerning the second principle: the redemption from that sin.[12] There are two common premises: (1) the physical punishment from that sin has still not been removed; (2) it is possible that the spiritual punishment can be removed.

There is disagreement concerning only one premise: the Christian says that the spiritual punishment was removed with the death of the messiah and the Jew denies that.

Concerning the third principle: trinity. There are seven common premises:[13] (1) God's existence is necessary, that is, His existence comes from Himself, not from anything else; (2) the divine quiddity[14] has all perfections eternally; (3) His simplicity is absolutely, infinitely simple; (4) He has in Him eternal life, power, wisdom, will, and other eternal perfections;[15] (5) there is no internal inconsistency in Him; (6) He is not subject to composition at all; (7) there is nothing in God, may He be blessed, which is not divine. There is disagreement concerning three premises: (1) the Christian says God, may He be blessed, has three separate attributes, which he calls Persons,[16] and the Jew denies this; (2) the Christian believes that God, may He be blessed, has an attribute called Son, generated from the Father, and the Jew denies this; (3) the Christian believes that God, may He be blessed, has an attribute which proceeded from the Father and the Son called Spirit, and the Jew denies this.

Concerning the fourth principle: incarnation.[17] The Christian believes that the Son took on flesh in the womb[18] of the virgin. This incarnation was indivisible and inseparable in the same unity and even greater than the conjunction of the human soul to man, such that even after he was crucified and died, the divinity remained conjoined to and united with the flesh and the soul, namely with each one separately. The Jew denies all of this.

Concerning the fifth principle: virgin birth.[19] The Christian belief is that at no time was the virginity rent, not during the birth, not before the birth, and not after the birth. The Jew denies this.

Concerning the sixth principle: transubstantiation.[20] The Christian belief maintains that when the priest says special words, at the very instant when he finishes his statement,

God, the incarnate Son, is in the dimensions of the wafer[21] and the wine in the same quantity and in the same glory which the Christian thinks he has in heaven.[22] The Jew denies this.

Concerning the seventh principle: baptism. The Christian belief maintains that he who has not been baptized has no portion in the world to come.[23] The Jew denies this.

Concerning the eighth principle: the coming of the messiah. The common premise is that the prophets predicted his coming. We disagree about the time of his coming, for the Christian says he has already come, while the Jew denies this.

Concerning the ninth premise: a new Torah. There is one common premise: the previous Law still exists. There is disagreement concerning three premises:[24] (1) The Christian says that all the commandments except for the Ten[25] are statutes[26] and it is not proper to observe them. The Jew says that it is proper to observe all the commandments forever, and nothing has been added on to them. (2) The Christian maintains that their new Law perfects the previous one, and the Jew denies this. (3) The Christian says that our previous Law did not give perfection or eternal life to the soul until the advent of the new one, which does give those things to people who walk in its ways. The Jew says that the previous Law gives eternal life, and nothing has been added on to it.

Concerning the tenth principle: demons.[27] They agree about one [premise]: [demons] exist. They disagree about another: the Christian says that they were good angels who sinned at the beginning of their existence through pride and jealousy and, at the very same instant, their free will was removed from them and they became wicked. The Jew denies all this.

After these premises have been set forth in every one of the principles, it is proper that we posit a few general premises which we shall need in this polemic so that this treatise will be more perfect and the desired end, namely establishing the truth, will be clearer and more manifest.

Let me say that the general premises are three: (1) faith will not force the intellect to believe something which leads to a contradiction; (2) one cannot imagine that the divine power is able to contradict either the first intelligibles[28] or the derivative principles which have been clearly and absolutely demonstrated, since they derive from the first intelligibles;[29] (3) divine justice seeks good for mankind and leads it to the greatest perfection possible with respect to its nature,[30] as it is written, "For our good always."[31]

After all this has been stated, it is proper to understand that which will be included in this treatise. It will be divided into ten chapters according to the number of principles. We shall speak in utmost generalization and brevity, eschewing all verbosity. It is proper, however, that one self-evident assumption should preface this endeavor: if the demonstrative proofs and evidence of the two parties, though conflicting, are of equal value such that no advantage can be found for either one, then the party of the Hebrews has the established claim of truth[32] since it is presumed to have the divine Law. Since faith is the most exalted of matters, it is proper that they not be removed from their established claim of truth except through great arguments and strong demonstrative proofs ensured against all doubt.[33]

Now that we have finished this Preface, we wish, with the help of God, to explain the chapters clearly. Even though the Christian belief has been clarified in this introduction according to the premises which have been set forth, it is my wish to repeat and clearly explain it in every one of the chapters, so that we shall be safeguarded against any error or equivocation.

CHAPTER
1

Concerning the Punishment
of Adam's Sin[1]

The magnitude of a sin is calculated according to the importance and stature of the sinner. One also examines the sin in regard to the stature of the offended party, so that its gravity and magnitude are according to his stature.[2] It is, therefore, proper that a sin will be calculated as greater and more marvelous when committed by a perfect man, not predisposed to sin, with no inclination toward transgressions,[3] especially if this man received favor and grace from the offended party.[4] Adam's sin and rebellion were made against God, may He be blessed, Who is infinite in His stature. The sin was perpetrated by a man predisposed to perfection, one who was the least naturally inclined to sin that one could possibly find. This is the case, since [Adam] was the work of [God's] hands and received from Him, may He be blessed, the most perfect grace and favor that human nature can receive, for he was created perfect in his species.[5] For all these reasons, the Christian says that his sin was enormous and infinite, since it potentially included the whole of mankind, which came after him and emerged from him.[6] As a result, they think it is proper and correct that the punish-

29

ment be infinite and include all of mankind and that this species properly deserves an infinite punishment. It is even more proper that grace, mercy, and favor, namely eternal life and pleasure, be removed from mankind,[7] since, in truth, justice demands that the pleasant eternal life cannot be achieved through commandments or forms of worship,[8] without the addition of divine grace and mercy, as is maintained by the theologians.[9] Since the matter is so, it is clear that the human species would not suffer a miscarriage of justice were it lacking this grace and favor. This matter is properly conceived thus according to the Christian intention in this first principle.[10]

Now it is proper to explain clearly the refutations and doubts which follow from this belief both with respect to speculation[11] and with respect to scriptures, with those of speculation first.

We say: There are four arguments against the propriety of this opinion.

I. First, we deny that premise which states that justice demands that paradise[12] and eternal life cannot be achieved by means of worship[13] without divine grace. Instead, we maintain that he who worships God can achieve [this reward] naturally by means of his speculative life, which causes pleasure to his holy soul, so that he inherits eternal life. It is proper to maintain this position.[14] Since the facts are as they have been posited, denying this pleasure from souls is not merely a denial of favor and grace, but, rather, it is an infinite punishment. But inflicting an infinite punishment on Noah's soul,[15] which has no connection with, or dependence on, Adam's soul, would be a great divine injustice, God forbid.

II. Even if we should posit the above premise, for the sake of argument, even though it is not true, I say that the removal of grace and favor from one who does not deserve to have them removed is not divine equity. The souls of the righteous, such as Noah and the patriarchs, peace be upon them, have no connection with the sinning soul of Adam, especially since, according to the Christian belief, each person's soul is created by God, may He be blessed, for each particular body.[16] Therefore, they did not sin, and it is not proper that infinite grace and mercy be removed from them.[17]

III. I say further: If Adam, before he sinned, was worthy of grace and mercy and would have inherited eternal pleasure, [certainly] Abraham and the rest of the righteous men were more worthy of receiving this grace. This follows from what I say: If Adam, who was born perfect, not predisposed to sin, would have acquired this grace, then Abraham, who was born in sin and conceived in iniquity,[18] yet did not sin but instead lived an exemplary and blessed life, would be more worthy of pleasure since his stature is more apparent and praiseworthy. Therefore, it would be divine injustice for Adam to inherit pleasure if he had not sinned, despite his low stature, while Abraham, who did not sin, even though conceived in iniquity,[19] would lose his eternity despite his high stature as a man whose thoughts did not tempt him nor his ideas lead him astray from worshipping God out of love.[20]

IV. If divine equity seeks for mankind the greatest good and guides it to the most wondrous perfection which can be received, as was posited in the introduction to this treatise,[21] how can it follow that God would remove His grace and truth from him who has not sinned against Him and from whom it is not proper to remove it? Where is His former mercy[22] for mankind if this were true? Furthermore, the punishment of souls is not merely denying them the pleasure of paradise[23] but also causing them pain and suffering and sending them to perdition in Hell.[24] The soul may be naturally bereft of God's grace, but at least it is not in painful sorrow and blown by fire.[25] It can, by means of its intellection while still in its body, possibly acquire participation with the separate intellects from which the soul is formed and which are of its nature.[26] How could God descend from His glorious throne to punish such a soul which naturally has this [reward] and put it in Hell? Shall not the Judge of all the earth deal justly?[27] Far be it from God to do such injustice!

These are the doubts which follow from this presupposition with respect to speculation, not including those remaining from the second principle which will be dealt with there. [Those arguments] which follow from Scriptures [are dealt with] in the ninth principle, in which we shall explain clearly beyond any doubt that the Torah of Moses gives eternal life.

Now, however, we shall offer a proof whose truth is obvious, namely, that the theologians admitted that because of one simple easy commandment, i.e., circumcision, with which Abraham, peace be upon him, was commanded, much of the spiritual punishment was removed from him, because the punishment of Hell was removed from him,[28] even though he was not brought into the inner part of the sanctuary.[29] According to this proportion, the Torah of Moses, peace be upon him, which contains 613 perfect commandments,[30] should properly be able to remove even more of the spiritual punishment from souls and to give them some rest.[31] There is an even more reprehensible [consequence]: why should the souls of the prophets who beheld the glory of God while still in their bodies (especially Moses our Teacher, peace be upon him, about whom Scripture testifies: "The Lord would speak to Moses face to face, as one man speaks to another;[32] and he beholds the likeness of the Lord"[33] whenever he wanted[34]) lack this pleasure and intellection after death once the bothers of the body and the company of the senses had been removed, so that these pure, separate, intellecting souls remained, clean of any dross or rust? It is not proper to ascribe this to divine equity. This is what we have to say in this first chapter.

Concerning Redemption from
Adam's Original Sin
Called in their Language
"Original"

Since the gravity of a sin is estimated according to the offended party, the stature of the sinner, and the sin itself, as has already been explained,[1] a man soiled by that particular sin would not be sufficient to redeem it. This is the reason, the Christian thinks, that the divine wisdom and mercy agreed to receive human flesh so that the death of this completely perfect, unblemished man would redeem [mankind] from the enemy, and spiritual punishment would be removed from human souls. This is the conceptualization of their belief in this second principle.[2]

The refutations which follow from this belief are of three kinds: (I) this redemption is not necessary; (II) this redemption is not relational and proportional; (III) this redemption is not possible.

I. I say: If the spiritual punishment of the sin of Adam did not pass to the soul of anyone other than Adam himself, as we explained in Chapter 1, it follows that this redemption is not necessary. We say further that even if we posit that it

is possible that the spiritual punishment passed to all souls,
this redemption is not necessary. This becomes clear when
we posit the obviously true premise that Divinity has no
relation or proportion with anything else.[3] After that, we say
that if because of the blood of Abraham's circumcision, the
punishment of Hell has been removed from the souls, then
it is immeasurably more proper that the blood of the God-
man's circumcision will bequeath grace and favor to them
and will cause them pleasure.[4] It is obviously clear that such
a drop of blood as this would be sufficient, according to the
importance of his stature, to atone for the immeasurably
most important sin that could be imagined. This redemption would have been the most special one as we shall
clearly explain in this chapter.[5]

II. I say:[6] This redemption is neither proportional nor relational. I posit that which their sages have posited in this matter.
They say that it is proper that the redeemer give something for
that which he wishes to redeem.[7] We then say that the redemption of sin is neither proportional nor relational in the absence of
worship[8] or justice. This redemption, however, was not by
worship and commandment and not with respect to justice;
therefore, it is not proportional.[9] That the conclusion follows
from the premise is obviously clear, since the removal of sin
without worship or without justice is called grace and not redemption. The contradiction of the conclusion [that is, the
second premise],[10] namely that this redemption was not by
worship and not by justice, is clearly explained as follows: The
death of the messiah was neither worship nor commandment,
since, according to Aristotle, *Ethics*, I,[11] these are applicable only
to voluntary actions: their sages admit this.[12] But death in its
human aspect is compulsory and necessary. Therefore, [Jesus'
death] was not [an act of] worship.[13] That it was not just is clear.
He was the only person not born in sin nor conceived in iniquity,[14] and it is neither proper nor equitable that one person be
punished for the sin of another.[15]

I say[16] further that redemption is impossible unless it is by means of the person himself who sinned or at least by means of someone of his species.[17] Thus, it is clear that it would be neither proper nor proportional and relational that an angel be punished for the sin of a man. But this man, the messiah, is more exalted than an angel;[18] therefore it is not relational and proportional that a man of this type should be punished. I say further that since this messiah is not of the human species, the punishment which he would suffer to redeem the sin of man is not proportional and not relational.[19]

III. I say: This redemption is impossible. We say: If incarnation is impossible, then this redemption is impossible; but incarnation *is* impossible; therefore this redemption is impossible. The necessary [truth] of the argument is obviously clear, and the contradiction of the [second] premise will be explained clearly in Chapter 4.[20]

I say further that even if we posit that God can become incarnate, this redemption is impossible. This is so because disease is cured by its opposite,[21] that is, sin with commandments, rebellion with worship. The curing of disrespect with a greater disrespect is curing rebellion with rebellion, and sin with sin. That the rebellion of a man who was potentially the whole species and who sinned against one easy commandment, namely, eating from the Tree of Knowledge, be cured with the rebellion against God's essence[22] by the nation which the Lord chose from among all other peoples on earth[23] is apparently the greatest injustice that could possibly be imagined in all of nature, let alone by a God who is most perfectly righteous and equitable.

I say further that since it is posited that God directs all men to their perfection and to the greatest good which they could receive by their nature,[24] then if this redemption were possible, it would necessarily make the exalted and choicest part of mankind into something dirty and abominable.[25] It is clear from all of this that if there were a need for redemption from that sin, it would have been more proper and special that it be with the blood of his circumcision, since [circumcision] is in itself a commandment and a form of worship, and it would have been sufficient according to the stature of his glory.[26]

I say further that it is very reprehensible to say that in order to remove the general sin of this species which was properly punished, [humanity] was given majestic splendor instead of afflictions. This follows from their statement that Divinity became incarnate in human flesh such that the whole human species became greatly glorified[27] and, in His death, [God] did not cause the masses to feel afflictions or pain at all.

It follows from all this that this redemption is impossible. This is what is proper to posit with respect to speculation concerning these principles. In Chapter 9 it shall be clearly explained that the Torah of Moses our Teacher, peace be upon him, is a heritage of eternal life , and, therefore, before [Jesus'] death, [mankind] enjoyed pleasure, and, so, there was no need for [this redemption].

CHAPTER

3

Concerning the Trinity

The Christian belief posits that the divine substance en-
compasses three attributes, *personas* in their language, and
one quiddity. [The attributes are] Father, Son, and Holy
Spirit, or power, wisdom, and will. The Father generates the
Son, and, from the love of both, the Holy Spirit proceeds.[1]
The Father is the power, the Son is the wisdom, the Spirit is
the will. The three are in quiddity one God. They are
distinct, but [only] as attributes, and each one of them is
God. This is their belief in this principle.[2]

Although the doubts and the refutations[3] which follow
from this belief are many and of different kinds, all cause
contradiction to and denial of the common premises which
were posited in this principle.

I. This belief contradicts the first premise, which states
that God, may He be blessed, has necessary existence.[4] We
say: If the Son were generated, then God would be generated. This follows from your statement that each one of
them is God. If God were generated, then He would be an
effect. This is clear since the generator is the cause of his
existence. But someone who is caused cannot have necessary existence. This is clear because such a being would be

37

dependent [on something else]. It would follow, therefore, that God could not have necessary existence.[5]

We shall offer a similar proof concerning the Holy Spirit. We say: The Holy Spirit proceeds; therefore, God proceeds; therefore, God is an effect; therefore, He does not have necessary existence.[6] According to these two arguments, this belief contradicts the first common premise.

II. Against the second common premise, namely, God has all the perfections eternally,[7] I say: The Father was not perfect until he generated the Son, since previously he was in potentiality. Therefore, he was brought from potentiality to actuality. Therefore, all the perfections were not eternally in Him.

I say further: If the Father generated the Son, this was either in time or instantaneously.[8] But this could not have been in time, because in the first half of the time in which he was generated, he did not exist; and, then, he would have existed only after nonexistence.[9] He would, therefore, not be eternal, the opposite of what has been posited.

The only alternative, therefore, is instantaneous generation.[10] But it could not have been in one single instant, because the exact same refutation would follow, namely that he existed after not existing, because before that particular instant, he did not exist. Therefore, he would not be eternal.

There is no other alternative, therefore, than that the Father generates him continuously in consecutive instants, and he receives his existence from [the Father] continuously without there being a first instant from which his existence began. Hence, the Father is the agent of the Son, continuously, in every instant, eternally. Just as the Father is eternal, so, too, is the Son who receives existence from him eternal, being generated in every single instant.

Refutations pointing to reprehensible consequences follow from this [doctrine]. First, time would be composed of instants and moments, since [the Son] is generated[11] from [the Father] continuously in every single instant. The impossibility of this notion has already been clearly and absolutely demonstrated in *Physics* IV and VI, namely, that time is continuous and is not composed from that which is indivisible, and it is not composed of moments. Rather, it is potentially divisible infinitely as any other continuous magnitude.[12]

It is fitting that you know that the Christians believe in [the logical conclusion of] this preceding disjunction, namely that [the Son] is continuously generated and that the Father generates the Son continuously. Just as there is no first or beginning for the Father, there is no beginning or first for his action, namely, this Son. [The Father] causes [the Son] to exist continuously.[13] It follows that time must be composed of instants, since [the Father] cannot generate [the Son] in continuous time, but in an instant, and [the Son] receives existence from [the Father] continuously, and [the Son] exists from [the Father] in every single instant. Hence, time would be composed of these instants.

Furthermore, a more serious refutation follows from this premise, namely, the Son is destroyed continuously. This is because they claim that he receives existence from the Father and follows from him in every instant continuously. If [the Father] generates him in one instant and his existence is perfected, then it is impossible that he cause him to exist by generating him a second time. The perfect thing, namely, that thing which exists in actuality, cannot be brought into existence a second time unless it has ceased to exist, and [only] after it has ceased to exist, can it come into existence or be generated another time. Since you claim that the Son is generated continuously and follows from the Father continuously, it follows that he will cease to exist continuously in every instant. Then he will come into existence and then he will cease to exist and then he will come into existence continuously, infinitely, and eternally.

A more serious refutation follows from this, namely, that [the Son] both ceases to exist and exists in every instant, such that in one instant he exists and does not exist. This is clear from your saying that [the Son] receives existence from [the Father] continuously. Now the thing which exists is not generated until it ceases to exist. Yet, [the Father] generates him in every instant. Therefore, in every instant [the Son] ceases to exist, for if he would last even one instant, [the Father] could, therefore, not generate him continuously, since in that same instant in which he would remain existent, he would not be generated, because the existent cannot come into being or be activated while it still exists. Therefore, he must cease to exist in every instant so that he can receive existence every instant. Since this is true, it is clear that in every instant he will be coming into being and ceasing to exist, existing and nonexisting. This is clearly false.

It would follow, therefore, that God the Son who exists now is not the same one who existed yesterday, and not even in the past instant, since that Son has already ceased to exist and this one exists.

Many other refutations pointing to reprehensible consequences follow from this besides the first refutation which applies to them, namely, since God the Son is an effect of the Father, he is not perfect. This is the opposite of what was posited in the premise that all the perfections are eternally in Him.

Similar contradictions can be made to the procession of the Holy Spirit, namely that [the Spirit] proceeds from [the Father] in time or in an instant, and then all the refutations which follow from the generation of the Son [would apply]. This is self-evident.

This is how the words of the Rabbi, of blessed memory, should properly be understood in this place. I expanded the explanation in my translation, since his language is brief and recondite in this place, and I have seen no one who could understand it. Hence, I transgressed the rules of translation here more than in the other chapters.[14]

Joseph said: This rabbi formulated this contradiction to the Christians from that which Al-Ghazali[15] wrote in the first section, question four, of *The Incoherence of the Philosophers*,[16] as completed by the sage Rabbi Levi ben Gershom in book 6 of his book *The Wars of the Lord*.[17] He[18] said that if the world is emanated[19] from the Creator and He is the agent of it, then it follows that He cannot be the agent of it continuously; and it cannot be emanated and follow from Him continuously. If this were so, then time would be composed of instants, and the heavenly bodies would cease to exist continuously, and they would cease to exist and come into being at every instant, in the very same way which we have made clear concerning the generation of the Son, if it were continuous. Since it has been made indubitably clear that the world, that is, the matter of the spheres and their stars and the earth, exists by virtue of an agent and an agent has caused it to be,[20] it is impossible that this be continuous, according to that which has been posited. It follows that they were made at one single instant and that they were brought into existence after nonexistence. Hence, he explained with this demonstrative proof that the world was created.[21] Similarly, if the Son received his existence from the Father, but not continuously, then he was brought into existence after nonexistence and he was created, the opposite of that which was posited, namely, that he is eternal.

He said further that it is impossible to conceive an effect continuously emanated[22] from its very beginning, unless it is something which quickly ceases to exist, in which no two parts remain together. This is the case of motion, which proceeds one part after another and is continuously composed of potentiality and actuality, and the actuality preserves the potentiality. This is why it is defined in *Physics* III as a certain potential entelechy[23] from the aspect of potentiality.[24] The matter is the same with respect to emanation[25] of light. But things which are substances, which are of a permanent nature, how could it be conceived that they are emanated continuously? How could it be conceived that the matter of the sphere is emanated continuously?[26]

The only alternative, therefore, is that [the world] exists from its beginning in one instant. This is the instant in which it received its existence after not existing. This is why Al-Ghazali said that the thing which exists does not need a cause of existence but needs a preserver of its existence; one cannot conceive a giver or agent of existence for something which already exists. Now since all the philosophers admit and have provided demonstrative proofs that the matter of the sphere and the number of the stars and its spherical nature and their condition are an effect, and that their existence is from something other than themselves, and that this cannot be continuous;[27] it follows that God, who created them after nonexistence, caused them to exist in the first instant. Therefore, they are absolutely created. This is his decisive demonstrative proof for the creation of the world. No one, even at first glance, can remove himself from this conceptualization, nor can he deny it, unless he does not know the nature of demonstrative proofs or he possesses great lust.[28]

This rabbi copied [the argument] here to use against the Christians concerning the generation of the Son and the procession of the Spirit. Therefore, he must have changed his mind, since he had already argued against this demonstrative proof in his book *Light of the Lord*.[29] I imagine that he composed this treatise after he had composed that book.[30] If this were not the case, then we have here deception, not demonstrative proof. This, however, would be inhuman and contrary to that which he intended as he mentioned in his premises.[31] Now, it truly appears that the arguments which he framed there are very weak, and I have already shown their weakness to the intelligent people of our nation. I discussed the truth, showing that he was not able to destroy the demonstrative nature of this proof and that he, of blessed memory, did not fully understand there the intentions of those who propounded this demonstrative proof until this very place.[32] I have already explained this clearly in a separate treatise which I composed on this subject.[33]

Joseph said: When I researched the matter further I saw[34] that Averroes[35] was somewhat sensitive to this argument. Hence, he said in many places that the world's existence is through motion, and he who gives motion, gives existence.[36] He said also that [the world's] existence is in its unity, and, therefore, the giver of its unity is the agent of it.[37] I imagine that he said this in order to avoid saying that God is always the agent of the bodies of the world, since it is clear that existing things cannot be created more than once. Hence, he attributed agency to motion which is continuously emanated from the Mover. Hence, the Creator, may He be praised, is not essentially the agent of the world, but of motion, which continuously needs a mover. As a result, the existence of the world is through motion, and the agent of the motion is the agent of the sphere, and, in this manner, [Averroes] decided to call Him "agent."

I saw that he said in his *Middle Commentary to Metaphysics*, XI, concerning separate intellects and how they originated, that there is no Agent but rather Thinker, Thinking and Thought, that which perfects and that which is perfected.[38] Furthermore, I saw him say in *The Incoherence of the Incoherence*, by way of doubt,[39] that it is possible to think that the world would not pass into nonexistence with the nonexistence of its cause, since it is considered a substance with qualities. This cannot be the case, however, in the case of the separate intellects, which exist by virtue of their ability to cognize their cause and which are counted by their relationship with each other.[40]

I saw further in *On the Heavens*, II, something which will contradict [Averroes'] intentions [concerning the eternity of the world]. It was made clear there that the form of the world and the number, position, and direction of the stars exist for some purpose and are the work of an agent.[41] Therefore, the question reverts to that which it was previously. Averroes in his wisdom tried to run away and hide and did not know what to do, as if the nature of truth forced him[42] to believe in creation, but he was seduced by the argument of Aristotle for the preexistence of the world. He thought that they were true demonstrative proofs, and he offered proofs which contradict the doubts; he tried to solve them, once this way, once that way. But he could not escape, since the truth shows the way.[43]

Now that this has been settled, we shall return to our previous activity, namely translating and explaining clearly the words of the sage, since this is not the place for this question. Still, we saw fit to clarify it here for the benefit which follows from it, for we found it agreeing with that which this sage explained clearly in this premise against the Christians. He said:

III. The third premise,[44] namely, that the divine quiddity has eternal life, power, wisdom, will, and many other perfections.[45] I say: If they posit that power, wisdom, and will are three separate attributes, that is, *personas*, then either we should posit life as a separate attribute, and, thus, it will follow that there will be more perfections and many attributes, not just three *personas*;[46] or it follows that He has none other than these [three] and is not alive. This is contrary to that which was posited in this premise, namely, He has eternal life.

IV. Concerning the fourth premise: God, may He be blessed, is infinitely simple.[47] Infinite simplicity means that there is no greater simplicity, since it is impossible that one infinite be greater than another.[48] But one can imagine a simplicity greater than the one which they have posited. This is clear since it is possible to imagine that He does not have multiple attributes, or that one attribute is God, and another attribute is God. It follows, therefore, that He is not infinitely simple. Furthermore: since the quiddity is other than the attributes, which is clear because the quiddity is one and the attributes many, it follows that He has four things, one quiddity and three attributes, not merely a trinity. This is against the premise which states that God is infinitely simple.

v. Concerning the fifth : God has no composition.[49] I say: Since it is clear that the attribute and quiddity are different, as we have mentioned;[50] and it is also clear that the attribute will either generate or spirate[51] and the quiddity neither generates nor spirates;[52] therefore, He is composed of quiddity and attributes, subject and predicate. This is opposite that which has been posited in this premise.[53]

Joseph said:[54] Aristotle mentioned in *Metaphysics*, VI, that a thing and its quiddity are one thing, and the universal intelligible quiddity is the thing in actuality, and this is other than a thing in potentiality.[55] Thus, the intelligible quiddity of Reuben is Reuben in actuality but is other than he in the sense [that it relates] to other individuals, namely, it can be predicated of every individual of the species. But the individual quiddity found outside [the intellect] is the man himself.[56] As to this divine quiddity, which is one in the Father, Son, and Spirit, if it is a universal intelligible quiddity, then it is necessarily subject to definition and is compound. It follows that there must be three [separate substrata] of matter on which the multiplicity is dependent, as I have explained in my *Commentary to the Epistle* of En Profiat. If it is an individual quiddity, then that which has the attribute will itself be the attribute, and the quiddity of the Father will be the attribute of the Father, and there will be no multiplicity in the attributes as there is no multiplicity in the quiddity. This is opposite that which they posited, as I clearly explained there.[57]

There is also multiplicity in attributes, even though they say each one is God. Furthermore, they have posited that each one is separate and individuated in existence. Therefore, there will be as many divinities as the number of attributes, and there will be three divinities, not one God as they posited. Yet, they assemble together contradictory statements and say that they are three and each one is God, and He is one God, there is no other. Therefore, He is three and He is one. They also say that He is simple and afterward they say that He has quiddity and attributes; therefore, He is simple and not simple, one and many. And they say that the individual essence of the Father is the essence of the Son, and the Father generated the Son; therefore, he generated himself. In general, many primary contradictions follow. He said:

VI. Concerning the sixth which states that God, may He be blessed, has no internal inconsistency.[58] I say: If it is as they have posited, then necessarily He would have internal inconsistency, and, indeed, infinite internal inconsistency. First, there would be internal inconsistency in that the quiddity is without multiplicity and the attributes have multiplicity. Furthermore, they are inconsistent in that the Father generates the Son and the Son does not generate. They are inconsistent further in that the Father and Son spirate, and neither the Spirit nor any one of them by itself can spirate, and also they cannot spirate infinitely; therefore, they have infinite internal inconsistency.[59]

Joseph said: They posited that the Son is perfect in the same degree as the Father and that [the Father] passed on to [the Son] all his power. Now if [the Father] passed on to [the Son] the power to generate and [the Son] does not generate, and this is because of some impediment, then [the Son] is not perfect. If he did not want to generate, then the power was in vain. And if [the Son] does not have the power to generate, he is imperfect and not in the same degree of power as the Father. So how could the Son be perfect to the degree of the Father, and this Father gives him existence and he is caused by him, while the Father receives nothing from the Son? He said:

VII. The seventh premise: there is nothing in God which is not God.[60] I say: If God is one quiddity and three attributes, it follows that not one attribute by itself is God. This is clear, since if each attribute were God, each one would have to be one quiddity and three attributes. It would also follow for each one of the three attributes, and, thus, ad infinitum. It follows, therefore, that not every [attribute] is God. This is against the seventh premise.[61]

Joseph said:[62] The investigation of attributes is very recondite. Already the Rabbi, the Guide, dealt with this at length in the *Guide*, part I.[63] Al-Ghazali[64] and Averroes[65] argued about it vigorously in *The Incoherence* and *The Incoherence of the Incoherence*. This rabbi, of blessed memory, maintained essential attributes, and this is clear from his words in his book *Light of the Lord*.[66] You should know, however, that the upholder of essential attributes is not of this kind.[67] We have not found any other word more suitable for translating the word *persona* than "attribute," but they have different meanings. This is clear, for they say the Father generates the Son, but he who posits that God, may He be blessed, has power and wisdom does not think, God forbid, that power is the agent of wisdom nor that power is God, nor that wisdom is God. Likewise, when existence and unity are posited as essential things of God's quiddity, as posited by the Rabbi, of blessed memory, they are not the essential quiddity. Therefore, this presupposition is not liable to any of the difficulties which follow from the Christian belief, and the [holders of this doctrine] do not say that they are both three and one or any of the other reprehensible things and refutations. This is very clear.

I had to point this out to you since I have noticed that some scholars raised the same refutations with respect to this sage's opinion about essential attributes.[68] This is the reason why they understood neither the truth of his opinion nor the difference between the theories. Now, what misled them is the word "attribute" [*to' ar*], which is not a correct translation of *persona*. Others have translated it by *parzof*,[69] meaning that the Father appears in this manner,[70] and also the Son and Spirit. In truth, [*to' ar* and *persona*] do not mean the same thing. This misled the accusers of those who propound the theory of attributes. Further, since [the Christians] say that the *personas* are power, wisdom, and will, and those who maintain attributes say that He has power, wisdom, and will, it was thought that both have the same meaning. This is not so.[71]

The Rabbi, the Guide, of blessed memory, and all those who philoso-phized denied essential attributes in order to avoid the composition which follows from the existence of attributes, which is impossible for that which has necessary existence.[72] This rabbi, of blessed memory, thought to solve that doubt which follows from this supposition in his book *Light of the Lord*.[73] None of these doubts follows from [his theory] or from the fact that they said that God has power, wisdom, and will, since, for rational people, [these attributes] are understood as one [unit].[74] He said:

This is what we wished to mention in this chapter con-cerning the refutations which can be brought against them from speculation. As for Scriptures, this is a very broad matter, and, hence, we refrain from discussing it here.

CHAPTER
4

Concerning Incarnation[1]

Since man was close to God before his sin and faithlessness, and when he rebelled and transgressed His command, God, may He be blessed, moved an infinite distance away from him; it was by God's grace and mercy that, by means of an infinite union of divinity and humanity, man was to be restored to his previous state close to Him, may He be blessed, with the redemption from that sin. As a result, wisdom necessitated that God, the Son, would become flesh in the virgin's womb[2] and be united with man in an indivisible unity, even after his death.[3] This conjunction is even greater than the unity of the soul with the body,[4] such that [the Son] would suffer death and afflictions in order to redeem the original sin of mankind. This is the Christian opinion with respect to this principle.

The doubts which follow from this belief are in the first place all [the doubts] which apply to the belief in the trinity. This is clear since if there is no trinity, there is no Son; and if there is no Son, he did not become incarnate. Yet, we say even if we posit that the trinity is possible, still one can find doubts of two kinds concerning this principle: (I) with respect to the final cause,[5] and (II) the aspect of the formal cause.[6]

[We shall deal] first with respect to the final cause.[7]

I. Included here are all the refutations which follow from the first principle, original sin, and from the second principle, redemption. There is another refutation pointing to reprehensible consequences which follow when we posit a self-evident premise, namely that the giving of glory and honor is a thing which requires more grace than would be required for atonement or removal of sin. As a result, it is reprehensible and invalid that human nature, while in the state of original sin, would have so much grace that God would conjoin with it without the removal of that sin, and that that redemption be necessary to remove that sin. It would be more proper that divine mercy, which could produce this grace, uniting God with flesh and giving this honor and glory to the human species though it was in sin, should have been more capable of removing that sin, especially since that redemption was not done by one who was the proper one to do it, as stated previously in Chapter 2. This is adequate concerning the aspect of the final cause of incarnation.

IIA. As for the aspect of the formal cause, I say: Man's uniting with God is impossible since it would involve a contradiction.[8] This is clear since man is finite and God, may He be blessed, is infinite. Therefore, no other case is so replete with an affirmative and a negative.[9] We have already mentioned that God has no power over things from which a contradiction would follow.[10]

B. Second, if this unity were possible, it would follow that this person, in which they united, would be neither God nor man. Rather, he would be another substance, composed of these two natures.[11] This will be made clear by two proofs. 1) First, we say that this unity is either by composition, or by juxtaposition of place, or by blending or by [a union of matter] and form; namely, when different things unite, they will do so either by composition of the elements in the composed thing;[12] or by blending, for example, like wine and oil;[13] or they are conjoined in one place;[14] or by

form, as if you were to say that form and matter are conjoined and that this conjunction is formal.[15] [This union]
could not be by composition, since the incorporeal cannot
mix with a body, let alone divine nature with human nature. It also could not be by blending or juxtaposition of
place, because God cannot be in a place. The only alternative, therefore, is that [the union] must have been formal,
meaning, thereby, that man had the status of matter and
God the status of form. Since this composed thing must be
different in species from matter and form (for when many
things unite and become one, that one is different from
every one of those things), it follows necessarily that, as a
result, [God incarnate] would be neither God nor man, but
would be one [thing] composed of humanity and divinity.
This is clear to anyone who has learned physics.[16]

    c. Many other refutations would follow, namely (1) it
would follow that the divine substance, may He be blessed,
is mutable, since when it became a human form, it necessarily changed. This is a terrible mistake.

    Joseph said:[17] They cannot escape this doubt, which is the greatest that
can be brought against them, namely, that by God's taking on flesh and by
His uniting with man, He became a material, corporeal form. If He did not,
why do you say that He became united or He took on flesh? It follows
necessarily that He ceases being Himself and He ceases being God. This is
because God is incorporeal, but when He becomes a corporeal or human
form, He already stops being immaterial, having been made a nonimmate-
rial, corporeal force. When He ceases to be incorporeal, he ceases being
divine, which is His essence, since incorporeality is necessary for His
divinity, actuality, and quiddity. That which ceases to be cannot generate
itself, and, hence, He cannot afterward become a human or corporeal form.[18]

    Their sages run away and do not know what to answer,[19] uttering with
their mouths that He is immutable. Nevertheless, it follows necessarily
[from their belief] that He changes, because they say that [the Son] conjoined to humanity with a marvelous, indivisible conjunction, and even

when [the Son] died, the divinity remained conjoined with the flesh, and the divinity remained conjoined to the soul, too. When he was in his mother's womb,[20] the divinity was there in the womb conjoined with the flesh, divinity remaining conjoined and united. When he was crucified, one could justifiably say that God was crucified and died, even though He was not born and did not die with respect to being God. Still, one could justifiably say that God died because of His having become united, conjoined, and having entered the [human] quiddity.[21]

This conjunction was not conjunction of apprehension, as when the intellect unites with the intelligible,[22] because when he was in the womb, and sleeping, and died, he was not cognizing or apprehending, and it is also not said about this conjunction that the subject is identical with the object.[23] It is also not conjunction of existence as the conjunction of the mover with the sphere or the Active Intellect with the implantation of semen,[24] since in those cases, its existence and action are seen. As it says at the end of *Physics*,[25] God is in the outer sphere, because in that place is the beginning of motion, of which God is the agent and the mover, but that which is not a body is not in a place, as Averroes mentioned in his *Commentary* there.[26] This conjunction is also not a conjunction of connection and love, and not a conjunction of providence and guarding for the same reasons which we mentioned concerning [conjunction of] apprehension.[27]

The only alternative, therefore, is that this is a conjunction of form with matter,[28] and the power [given] to the body was, therefore, a material form. As a result, one could justifiably say that Jesus was God, that later he became a material substance, and that he destroyed his divinity. Now, it has already been clearly demonstrated that a thing cannot destroy itself, just as it cannot create itself. Even according to Averroes, who says that the Active Intellect is our form and that it is incarnate as a predisposition, so that with respect to itself it knows what is there, and with respect to its conjunction with us it learns what is here, as he clearly explained in *On the Soul*, III;[29] this is not the same conjunction which is posited as possible for God. One can never justifiably say at any time that we are the Active Intellect[30] or that [the Active Intellect] is man, or that it changed and became human form, just as they say that one can justifiably say that Jesus was the true God who created heaven and earth. They cannot justifiably say that Jesus is God unless God was part of his definition. This is clear because if the answer to the question, What is he? is God, and if God has entered his quiddity, then [Jesus] must necessarily be the place of the matter, or his form in which the genus and specific difference are conceived.[31] They will not say, however, that God is Jesus' matter or genus.

The only alternative, therefore, is that [God] is his form, and in this way we can say that Jesus is God. When they say that Jesus is man, humanity will have the status of matter and divinity, the status of form. Therefore, [God] is the material form of the body of Jesus. The Active Intellect, however, according to Averroes, is not part of the definition of man, neither his genus nor his difference. Instead the issue refers to conjunction of existence or conjunction of influence, even though Averroes' opinion about the hylic intellect is evidently worthless, as Gersonides has demonstrated with a vigorous refutation in his *Wars of the Lord*, I.[32]

When you examine all that we have clearly explained for you in this treatise, you will see all the lies and reprehensible things they have said about God. "They have spoken falsely of the Lord and have said 'Not He.'"[33] The righteous, of blessed memory, have been exceedingly careful to remark that in the verse "Who is like you, O Lord, among the mighty,"[34] the word "mighty" [*elim*] is written defectively,[35] so that it could be read, "Who is like you among the speechless?" They made God speechless, for He hears the curse and imprecation but is silent.[36] This is the essence of imprecation and curse. Oh, that I knew[37] who moves the heavens with this great motion which you see if the Mover is not incorporeal, but a bodily power who exists today bodily in the heaven, according to their opinion.[38] And they cannot say that the Son became incarnate, but the Father and Spirit remained in their divine power, since they say that divinity is indivisible. As a result, it follows, and they admit it,[39] that divinity took on flesh. Hence, the divinity wholly changed and destroyed its own incorporeal essence, even if they say the Father did not take on flesh and that he is God.

Look at this contradiction! How they have made Him one and many, divisible and indivisible. When you investigate the aspects with respect to which they say that He is one and many, mutable and immutable, and you investigate what follows from their root beliefs, you will see that they are things which are said but which have neither conceptualization nor reality.[40] It was concerning this that Maimonides said, in *Guide* I:71, that the Christian sages generated the Kalam.[41] As a result, it is clear that their science, which is called "theology," is really a science just of words,[42] namely, a science which cannot be conceived. Their doctrine exists only in words. But belief is not that which is said but that which can be conceived. Even false belief must be capable of conceptualization, not merely stated with words, as he, of blessed memory, mentioned in a chapter of that part.[43] Therefore, this belief is worse than being simply false.

I have now clearly explained for you all the types of conjunction that can be imagined concerning incorporeal things. I have taken some of them from the beginning of Averroes' *Epitome of On the Soul*;[44] and some from that which he clearly explained in *The Epistle on the Possibility of Conjunction*;[45] and some from that which can be properly conceived in the Torah and the metaphysical and physical sciences. When you go over this note, you should use [these types of conjunction] in any place where it is proper, and you should not become confused.

Joseph said: A spirit went forth from God, and it became a lying spirit in the mouth of their sages,[46] and it forced them to say that God destroyed His divine incorporeal self and became a corporeal form or a corporeal force, and they did not even realize [what they were saying]. This is clear from their statement that God remained conjoined to the dead flesh while it was on the cross and united with it[47] such that one could justifiably say, "God was crucified."[48] If this conjunction were with divinity, then there was divinity in his divinity, and Jesus must have been alive. This is very clear since when a soul, which does not have the true divine life which divinity has, as has been clearly explained in Book Lambda [of the *Metaphysics*],[49] is conjoined with a body, then the person is alive. Now if the soul in its conjunction with the body gives it life, then true life, which is God, may He be blessed, more properly gives life to the body when it is conjoined with it,[50] since that which imparts a particular attribute to something is more truly characterized by this attribute. Aristotle has already used this premise in this manner in *Posterior Analytics*, I, and *Metaphysics*.[51] But, despite all this, according to their doctrines, [the flesh] was dead. It follows, therefore, that in this conjunction, God could not have remained in His divinity which has incorporeal, happy life. Rather, He destroyed His divine self and became a material force taking on flesh, and He died.

This, indeed, would be the proper consequence [of the incarnation], since His "life" refers to His intellectual apprehension, and to His abstract, incorporeal, and pure essence. If He became a bodily force, He would not have been able to apprehend Himself, because the apprehension of the essence of a thing is specifically done through an intellectual, incorporeal, pure, abstract conceptualization. This is the case whether we abstract it ourselves, as in the case where the intellecting comes out of the object, or whether it is in and of itself abstract and intelligible, as is the case of incorporeal things.[52] The truth of this concept has already been clearly explained in *On the Soul*, III,[53] and Aristotle explained it clearly in *Metaphysics*, XI,[54] namely, God, may He be blessed, apprehends because He is incorporeal, and He lives because He apprehends. According to the contrary of the contradictory,[55] it follows that a corporeal force cannot be conceived as an intellectual concept. He, therefore, does not live the special divine life, so in this type of conjunction He would die, since He would be there conjoined on the level of one of the elemental powers, which are corporeal forces. Now that this is clearly explained, we return to what we were doing, namely, translating the points made by the sage. He said:

It follows further that if [Jesus] was neither man nor God, then a man did not suffer death and afflictions; hence, the redemption was not by means of a man.[56]

2. The second argument:[57] If from the conjunction of soul and body one indivisible substance is made, then the conjunction of God with flesh, which they claim is a greater conjunction than that of the soul with a body, should properly make one indivisible substance. This is clear because that which follows from a lesser conjunction should properly follow from a greater conjunction. Then, all the aforementioned refutations follow.

3. The third argument: If this unity were possible, it would follow that the Son changed to two essences at one instant at the time of his death, as he united with the soul and united with the dead flesh. Each one of these two conjunctions made one essence, but it is impossible for the essence which comes from the unity of divinity with the soul to be the same essence which comes from the unity with the flesh.

4. The fourth argument: The unity with the flesh at the time of death was not the divine unity with a man, since when the soul separates from the flesh and dies, it cannot justifiably be said to be "man," nor defined as "rational animal."

5. The fifth argument: This unity, which they claimed is indivisible, is separable and divisible. This occurred when he died, because then there was no conjunction of divinity and humanity. Even though they say that He remained conjoined with the soul by itself, and the body by itself, still this unity is already separable, namely, the unity of God with man. Things which can justifiably be said about separate things cannot be attributed to compound things. Unity of God with man happens when He unites with him when he is alive, when the soul and flesh are together. When, however, they separate at death, one cannot justifiably say that they are man. Hence, [God] did not stay conjoined with man, and, hence, the divine conjunction was separated from the human nature, which is the opposite of what they posited when they said that at no time was this conjunction separated. Oh, that I knew[58] what kind of essence comes from the conjunction of God with dead flesh, and how this conjunction is possible! This is what can be said in this chapter with respect to speculation.

III. With respect to the Torah. We say exactly what the prophet Isaiah said when he condemned Pharaoh for believing that he had divine emanation: "The Egyptians are men, and not God; and their horses are flesh, and not spirit."[59] It follows that this refutation applies to them, since we say that Jesus was a man, not God, for it is impossible to be a man and God; as Isaiah, peace be upon him, said. With respect to the Gospels, I say: If [Jesus] was essentially a man, he would be obligated to observe the Torah of Moses. Even if the divinity were conjoined with him, he would have this obligation because he would still have been a man. So, he should not have said to his mother, "Female, what do you want, etc."[60] These arguments contradict that which was posited in this principle.

Concerning Virgin Birth

We have already explained clearly in the Preface the Christian belief, namely that the virginity was neither rent nor destroyed at any time, neither before the birth, nor during the birth, nor after the birth.[1]

The argument which contradicts this is very evident and follows from an obviously clear presupposition, namely that it is impossible for a body to be without dimensions. This is so since dimensions are part of the definition [of body],[2] as is stated in the beginning of *On the Heavens*:[3] A body is that which has three dimensions, namely, length, width, and depth; the definition is congruent with the thing defined.[4] We then say: The sides of a virgin's womb[5] adhere to each other and have no dimensions between them. If a body were to pass between these sides, there would be dimensions, namely the dimensions of the passing body, and it would follow, therefore, that there were dimensions between [the sides]. But it has already been posited that there were no dimensions between [the sides]. This is an impossible inconsistency.[6]

If [the Christian] says that God can glorify a body such that it can pass through another body without dividing it, this is not an argument for one who seeks the truth. For [the Christian] transforms a problem into an assumption with a strange name, namely, that there is a glorified body, which they call *glorificado*.[7] They cannot mean that there is a body without dimensions, because, therefore, it would be a body and not a body. If it has dimensions it cannot pass through something without dimensions, as is the case with the sides of a virgin's womb. It is clearly contradictory for something to have dimensions and not to have dimensions. But if it were possible for this *glorificado* body to enter into another body, it would not lack dimensions, since dimensions are part of the definition [of body]. Instead, it would be as if the dimensions of this body entered the dimensions of the other body, even though this is absolutely impossible, because two cubits cannot be one cubit and the part cannot equal the whole.[8] And it would be possible that the whole world, despite its marvelous size, could enter into a grain of mustard seed.[9] Even if it were posited that this is possible, it would still be impossible for [a body] to pass between two bodies which have no space between them, because then there would be both space and no space. If this boy, who could not possibly be imagined to have passed between these parts since they were adhering to each other, did not pass between them, then there was no birth. Even if he passed through another place[10] and his dimensions entered into the dimensions of that body, it would not be called birth because he did not pass through the sides of the womb when they adhered to each other. This is clear from the definition of birth. This is what can be said about this principle from the aspect of speculation. In Chapter 9 we will say that which follows from the Torah.

CHAPTER
6

Concerning Transubstantiation[1]

The conception of the Christian belief has been clearly explained in the introduction to this treatise.[2] All the doubts which were raised about the trinity[3] and incarnation[4] refute belief in this principle. This is clear from their nature, for if the trinity does not exist, then there is no Son. If the Son does not exist, he did not become incarnate. If he did not become incarnate, he does not come to the altar. This is very clear.

But I say further that even if these principles are posited, this belief is refuted by the following arguments:

1. The first argument: I say, if God the incarnated Son were in the dimensions of the wafer[5] after the completion of the priest's statement, then either he was created there in the dimensions or he came there from outside the dimensions. Now, it is impossible that he be created there, since it would follow that God is created and ceases to exist, in addition to many other refutations.[6] The only remaining possibility, therefore, is that he must have come to these dimensions from the outside.

Other reprehensible impossibilities follow from this. First,[7] the statement of the priest is completed in an instant, and you say that in this instant he comes. There will exist, therefore, instantaneous motion,[8] let alone this great motion of an eight thousand year journey[9] from the place of his habitation[10] in the heavens to the earth. The contradiction of this has already been clearly demonstrated in *Physics*, IV and VI.[11] It is stated there that instantaneous motion is impossible, and in Book VI it is clearly explained that the distance in which there is motion and the time of the motion and the motion are equivalent, and they are infinitely divisible.[12] Just as the distance in which there is motion is posited to have a beginning and an end, so, too, does the motion in this distance have a beginning and an end. Time itself is nothing other than the measure of motion, according to the beginning and end which attach to its parts, all of which has been clearly demonstrated in that same book.[13] It has already been clearly explained in the introduction that there is no imaginable power that can change those things [whose impossibility] has been clearly demonstrated since [these demonstrative proofs] are derived from the first intelligibles.[14]

It follows also[15] that when he comes down from heaven to the altar and when he rises to the heavens after the wafer is eaten, the bodies of the heavens are rent. In fact, these are bodies which cannot possibly be rent or broken.[16] It would follow [from this doctrine] that [the Heavens] must be like tubes and orifices,[17] unless you say that he is a *glorificado* body[18] which can enter into the dimensions of the heavens without the heavenly bodies' being rent. This is one of those frightening things which are said but which have no reality and absolutely no intellectual conceptualization.

It follows also[19] that when it is said that God the Son remains in the heavens while he is in the hand of the priest, then he is in many different places at one time. Since we see him on thousands, and tens of thousands, and hundreds[20] of altars, then either there must be many divinities, or the very same body can be in many places at the same instant.

It follows also that in any place it is possible to create the Son of God and in any place it is possible to destroy him.

It follows also that when he rises to the heavens, the accidents, namely the qualities of the wafer — its color, odor, shape, taste, and the rest — will remain existing in themselves without a subject. This is against all nature or possibility.[21]

It follows also that these accidents can nurture. This can be seen through experience. If the priest eats one big wafer, he is nurtured, and the accidents become a substance, namely, his limbs, as is the case with all nutrients.[22]

I have already listed in my *Commentary on the Epistle* of En Profiat all the refutations and lies and reprehensible [consequences] which follow from this belief. I made it indubitably clear there that this principle disagrees with the precepts of all three sciences, namely, mathematics, physics, and metaphysics.[23] Consult it there or he who wishes to copy it let him copy it in this place.[24] He said:

Jeremiah has already said: "Can a man make gods for himself? No gods are they!"[25] And they make him every day. There is no difference between making him by hand or by word, since their priests believe that they make God by word when they say, "This is my body; this is my blood."[26] Look closely at how many marvels are in this marvelous statement which has this special quality to make God descend from the heavens. If, however, he remains there as they say, then, indeed, [the priest] makes [a god].[27] Job also said, "To him who brings God in his hand."[28] They bring this God in their hand and lift him up and lower him down and bring him to visit the sick, as you see them take and bring, raise and lower. They say he does not ascend or descend, nor does he go, but that he is in the dimensions of the wafer. But you see the dimensions ascending and descending and moving.[29] They, however, deny the sensibles just as they deny the intelligibles. They suffer reprehensible contradictions which they cannot escape. This is sufficient for this chapter.

CHAPTER
7

Concerning Baptism

The description of their belief has already been clearly explained in the Preface. The argument against it is as follows: It is clearly agreed that God is righteous and equitable. But this belief requires injustice with respect to Him, God forbid. Therefore, it is proper to uproot this principle.[1] This is clear after it has been posited that baptism works with a child according to the intention of the baptizer.[2] Suppose that there are here two boys, one the son of an evil rich person who has slaves and servants who arrange the baptism; the other one the son of a poor, perfectly righteous man, who has no helper and was unable to baptize his son despite his efforts.[3] Then the two boys die. How can the intention of the evil man save his son baptized for one day?[4] And how can a king sitting on the throne of justice punish the son of the poor person who did all he could, with the honesty of his heart, but was unsuccessful?[5] "Far be it from God that He should do wickedness, and from the Almighty that He should do wrong."[6] Ezekiel already said: "Sons shall not die for the iniquity of the fathers."[7] Hence, the divine justice will not punish the son for the bad quality of his father and his lack of effort at baptizing him.[8] This is sufficient for this chapter.

Concerning the Coming of the Messiah

The Christians say that the messiah has already come and the Jews deny this. Most of what can be said about this principle is scriptural, with very little from speculation. Nevertheless, we shall say something about it.

We say: If the messiah came for the purpose which, according to the Christian, was predicted [by the prophets], namely to redeem human nature, which, up to that time, was thoroughly dirty and polluted from that sin; then it is proper to think — and it is the truth — that the exalted status and the speculation which were part of the human species by means of the prophets and the high priests' Urim and Tumim at the time when [human beings] were impure and rejected because of that original sin, and at a distance from divine grace, should more properly be found at the time of their purification from this matter when they are close to God. But we have found nothing of this after his coming; rather, prophecy has departed, and the Urim and Tumim and the other divine matters have been missing since then.[1]

If they say that speculation and prophecy were necessary at that time to help the nations acquire correct belief, this is no answer. Speculation and prophecy were not merely to help the nation acquire belief, but for the perfection of the sages and the prophets, which in itself is a great perfection and a marvelous pleasure, since belief in itself is sufficient and continuous.[2] [Prophecy] was also intended to correct the leadership of the nation.[3] Today, there is an even greater necessity [for prophecy] in order to lead the Christian nation. Prophecy is necessary for them today to help them acquire belief and to preserve it, for today, in addition to other aspects of the Christian belief, they have had two leaders as Popes for approximately twenty years. Each one and his followers think the other is excommunicated and punished by Heaven, so that the necessity [for prophecy] is very great.[4]

Furthermore, it is very reprehensible that if the messiah came to cleanse original sin, especially of the chosen nation which he considered to be on the rank of sheep and the other nations on the rank of dogs, as stated in the Gospels,[5] that he leave them in confusion, panic, and great guilt, and especially the chosen nation of the children of Israel; and that he did not act in such a way so that he would be recognized by them and his mission verified for them, especially since original sin had already been removed. Why did he not show himself clearly and publicly,[6] since he admitted that his persecutors were mistaken, and he requested from his father that he forgive them?[7] This is now sufficient, since in the next chapter we shall speak more. When, however, we go over the prophecies we shall see that they hoped for things with the coming of the messiah which did not come and which were not seen when [Jesus] came: about the substance of the messiah, his family, the stature of his glory; about Jerusalem, Israel, the Temple, and universal peace for all nations; about life and the divine emanation, wisdom, prophecy, and the inclination to do good.

CHAPTER

9

Concerning the New Torah[1]

The Christian belief maintains three premises as was mentioned in the Preface of this Treatise.[2] (I) The first one: Their new Torah perfects and gives perfection to the Torah of Moses our Teacher, peace be upon him. Against this [premise] we shall make two arguments of two different kinds: (A) the first with respect to the Torah of Moses, and (B) the second with respect to their new Torah.

IA. The first argument. I say: If [the premise] were true, it would follow that the Torah of Moses, peace be upon him, is imperfect;[3] this is a great error. Therefore, the aforementioned premise is false. The logical consequence [of this syllogism] is obviously clear. If their new Torah gives perfection to the first one, then this first one, which receives the perfection, was not perfect until that one perfected it. The conclusion, namely, that the Torah of Moses is not perfect, is false,[4] and it can be contradicted as follows. Every activity has a specific proportion to its agent in regard to the level of the perfection, namely the perfection of the activity will be according to the perfection of the agent. Since the Agent of the Torah of Moses, peace be upon him, is fully perfect, it would follow that His activity, namely, the Torah, would be perfect to achieve its purpose, namely, the apprehension, love, and fear of God, as has been explained clearly in many places. It follows that it includes every perfection for the purpose of achieving that goal, namely, His apprehension, worship, and love.[5]

Someone might think to answer us that it was perfect in proportion to those who received it,[6] who were then intellectually deficient and far from perfection. They had become like animals because of their work for the Egyptians;[7] by being with [the Egyptians] continuously, [the Israelites] acquired their physical and terrestrial attributes, becoming insensitive to the spiritual. Hence, they needed external, physical things and promises of imaginary goods.[8] But after they were removed from these customs, acquired belief, and drew near to the spiritual values, the new Torah, which is fully and thoroughly spiritual, gave perfection to [their belief] and to their Torah.[9]

I think it is proper to explain clearly what is wrong with this answer with respect to reason and with respect to Scripture. At the time of Moses there was an increase in wisdom and the choicest of prophecy, both of which require a high level of intellectual and moral perfection. These qualities began to blossom with Abraham our Father, peace be upon him; they were transferred to the whole wise nation when they were in all of the Land of Egypt, and remained with them the whole time that their ancestors were there.[10] It was Abraham who recognized his Creator through prophecy and taught this publicly, and nations came to his belief,[11] and he called there on the name of the Lord, the Everlasting God.[12] It was he who tried to teach the way of the Lord to his children and his descendants as it is said: "I have chosen him, that he may charge his children and his household after him."[13] It can be assumed correctly that by learning the practices of Abraham, Isaac, and Jacob, their descendants were separated in Egypt and did not become involved with

Egyptian practices and teachings. If they had not maintained the tradition of their fathers and, in their youth, had
not held firmly on to their deeds and their teaching as an
inheritance, they easily would have chosen Egyptian man-
ners in order to escape enslavement. Why did they suffer
the great punishment and the exile and the persecution by
which the Egyptians imposed upon them heavy burdens?
Why did they not change their names,[14] and why did they
not join together to accept their evil counsel? Why did they
acquire the stature of closeness to God "to be a people for
His own possession, out of all the peoples that are on the
face of the earth?"[15] Add to this the public and continuous
miracles and marvels which they saw and felt, and the great
awesome things and favors they themselves received, as the
Master of the Prophets mentioned briefly in Deuteronomy:
"The great trials which your eyes saw."[16] Hence, it is clear
that one could not possibly find a nation possessing greater
predisposition to receive full perfection, being truly and
spiritually close to the Lord, than they were. It follows,
then, that clearly it is proper that the Torah of Moses should
have been fully perfect as is fitting for a divine law.[17]

In addition, when we review [the Torah's] details, we
shall see that its perfection is divine. We posit that the
human intellect is not always in actuality,[18] does not continuously have intellection, its matter rules its form, and
imaginary and physical lusts mislead it. It follows that a
divine law must posit not only religious principles but also
practical, speculative commands, which will break down the
luxuries of physical matters, will harmonize the powers of
anger and lust, and will give true and necessary opinions for
the perfection of man and his felicity.[19]

Since it has been made clear that it is proper that [these
qualities] should exist in a divine law, qua divine law, when
we review the Torah of Moses, peace be upon him, we
clearly see that it contains all of this. This points to the

Torah's full perfection and demonstrates that it sets this [perfection] as its goal, in its many positive and negative commandments, which are so plentiful that one neither slumbers nor sleeps[20] a material sleep. It arouses the eyes of the intellect, which wakes up in such a manner that it will not be enslaved by the will and the lusts. What becomes clear from all this is the validity of the Torah's perfect stature, as is proper for a divine law.

This can be seen further with respect to the singular quality in [the Torah] and the special advantage it has. The marvels, upon which [the Torah] is based, were the most publicized ones, even in the presence of those who disagreed. [They occurred] for a long period of time before sages who were great in the artifices and stratagems of the soothsayers.[21] Among these marvels, there are three special matters which cannot be duplicated in any other marvel recorded by another party, nor could they be of this nature. The preservation of this divine law is miraculous and it would not be possible if it were not a divine law.[22] This can be seen either in terms of the corporeal promises which are promised, or with respect to the religious commandments. [For example,] on the pilgrimage festivals, especially Passover, they needed protection, since men, women, and children made the pilgrimage. Thus, they were promised that their enemies would not harm them. The borders of the kingdom especially needed protection, since their inhabitants left them for the pilgrimage to the Temple; therefore, it says: "Neither shall any man desire your land, etc."[23] This was a continuous general miracle for the nation.[24] Similarly, concerning the sabbatical year, it says: "And if you say, 'What shall we eat, etc. . . . ,' I will command My blessing upon you in the sixth year, so that it will bring forth fruit for three years."[25] This is also a great, all-encompassing, continuous national miracle including both the rural and the common folk.[26] Similarly, [miracles occurred] in the investigation of a woman suspected of adultery who was made to drink the waters of the Sotah, in which God's name has been destroyed. This was a marvelous miracle — causing the body to swell and the thigh to fall away[27] — or if she were innocent she shall conceive children.[28] This is a marvelous miracle concerning a commandment, encompassing all people and times.[29] And there were continuous miracles and marvels done in our Temple.[30] All this clearly explains that observing this Torah, which Moses set before the children of Israel[31] by a miracle, [brings about] all the marvels and miracles, both hidden and manifest[32] before the eyes of the nations. These special properties can be found only in the divine law, namely, our law. All other conventional and divine laws are lacking and deprived of them and are far from this perfection. This is sufficient concerning this argument with respect to the holy Torah.

B. The second argument, with respect to their new Torah. I say: Not only is this Torah lacking and deprived of those perfections and special properties which were fully present in the earlier divine Torah, namely, those special things of a divine law; (it is clear that a law in which these things are not found could easily be conventional,[33] established by a human, relying on political philosophy or some other science);[34] but also, we say that when we look at the things included in [this new Torah], it will be found to be imperfect. This is clear with respect to many [aspects], first with respect to the contradictions found in it, and secondly with respect to the commandments.

1. Now to the contradictions with respect to the stories, and with respect to the proofs which can be offered from the stories. It says in the Gospels, "For with seventy-five persons their fathers descended to Egypt,"[35] but it says in Genesis, "seventy persons,"[36] and it counts there the number of persons which together added up to seventy. There is also a contradiction between the Gospel of St. Matthew[37]

and the Gospel of St. John about the family of Joseph, Mary's betrothed.[38] And in many places some parts contradict others.[39]

With respect to the contradictions in proofs, this is clear. St. Matthew in the Gospel makes a proof for Mary's being a virgin from Isaiah's statement: "Behold, a young woman shall conceive."[40] This is truly a great contradiction to the words of Isaiah, for he spoke there only to give a proof to Ahaz that he should not fear the two kings who arose against him. He gave a proof from this young woman, namely, how she would conceive and give birth to a son and call his name Emanuel,[41] as a sign that God would help them and protect them from the kings, before whom he was in dread. Ahaz lived five hundred years before Jesus,[42] so it is impossible for him to have been given a sign about this.[43] This is especially clear since Scripture says: "For before the child knows how to refuse the evil and choose the good, the land before whose two kings [you are in dread] will be deserted."[44] This is sufficient with respect to the contradictions.

2. Now, it is clear that [this new Torah's] teachings, commandments, and instructions[45] are deprived of all the choiceness and special characteristics which we have mentioned, so I will restrict myself to telling that which is in two of its chapters.

I say: in the Gospel of St. John, when [Jesus] desired to give stature to his Torah, he said: "From days of old it was commanded in the Torah, do not bear a grudge; I say: if your enemy strikes you on one cheek, give him the other one."[46] It is more proper that he be reproved, since he wished to criticize the divine Torah, which cannot possibly be defamed. If this is the correct instruction, then it would be more correct for the divine Torah to have commanded that. [One could not argue] that what prevented this [commandment] was their animal nature, namely, that it could be said that they were not ready for it. On the contrary, it is clear that they were ready for suffering and disgrace more then than they were at the time of Jesus' command, because at the time of Moses they were experienced with the burden of exile and sated with poisonous and bitter fruit,[47] while in [Jesus'] time they were free men, and kings shall see and arise[48] from them. Hence, it is clear that if this statement were perfect, it would have been included in the Torah of Moses, and if it were not [in the Torah of Moses despite its perfection], that would be a great imperfection in God's act, for it could not be due to a deficiency in those who received [the Torah], as we have made clear. It is absolutely true that [Jesus'] commanding this is a great deficiency, for the ultimate suffering is the absence of revenge. God ordered: "You shall not take vengeance;[49] you shall not hate your brother";[50] but to prepare oneself for degradation and shame is a criminal sin against ordinary love, for every man must love himself. [In doing this] he causes his fellow person to sin and to fail by giving him an opportunity to sin against him. Causing someone else to sin is a great sin, as is mentioned there.[51]

In that chapter[52] there is another mistake. He says there: "In the previous Torah, it is said: 'Love your neighbor and hate your enemy,' but I say 'Love your enemy'."[53] It is clear that the divine Torah does not command hating anyone except the enemies of God, as David, of blessed memory, praised himself, "Do I not hate them that hate You O Lord."[54] [The Torah] prohibits hating anyone other than enemies of God, for he who loves them is wicked. And if [Jesus] commanded to love them, why did the Torah command to hate them, and if [the new Torah] did not command to hate the enemies of God, then this command contained a great mistake.

I say further: Since the intention of the divine law is the guidance of people to bring them to felicity, then the law which easily guides them to perfection is more fully perfect. Since achieving perfection by means of this new belief is more difficult, it is, therefore, not perfect. This is clear because it posits that natural actions are mortal sins and reasons for excision of the soul; [these are] actions which are the custom of most people, the daily escape from which would be quite difficult for most of the world, such as anger and gluttony and laziness. For one such sin a man will be lost eternally. This is the worst and most reprehensible thing which could happen to someone.[55] This is what we wanted to say with respect to its instructions.[56] Here we have completed what we wanted to argue in the first premise of this principle.

II. We shall make the following arguments against the second premise, which says that all the commandments, except the Ten, are statutes which have no reason, they are not eternal, and it is not proper to observe them.[57]

A. First, since the divine Torah in its entirety is eternal and permanent, and it is proper to observe it, and its commandments are called Torah and its statutes are called Torah in general in many places,[58] it follows, therefore, that they are eternal also. If someone might think that the term "Torah" is equivocal, the true meaning referring only to the Ten Commandments, and only they are eternal, we would say that he must verify this opinion and bring proof for this equivocation. Rather, I say that the matter is clear: One cannot find in any place that the Ten are called Torah. Whenever the term Torah is used in general, it refers to all 613 commandments.[59] It is proper that it be understood as the Gospels say, that not even one drop will be taken away from the Torah,[60] in which "Torah" is not restricted to the Ten Commandments.

B. Second, it is proper to observe those commandments through which one is sanctified and called holy. But there are many commandments which are of this nature; therefore, it is fitting to observe them forever. This is clear in many places in Leviticus, especially concerning forbidden foods,[61] forbidden sexual relations,[62] and impurities,[63] so that you shall be holy, for I the Lord am holy.[64] It follows, therefore, that it is proper to observe these commandments. How could one not [observe them], since some of them keep animality and pollution away from man,[65] and they bring him close to the Lord of the world!

C. Third, since the reasons for some of the commandments, such as levirate marriage,[66] the holidays,[67] and others, are explicit, and [these reasons] are applicable forever, it follows that we must observe them according to their simple meaning.

D. Fourth, if the statutes are not forever because they point to some past or future event, then baptism is of this nature, because it points to purification of sin.[68] Therefore, [baptism] is a statute. Now, if it is proper to observe [baptism] according to its simple meaning, even though it points to something else and is a sign for something other than itself, why is it not proper that the statutes, even if we admit that they are a sign for something else, should be observed according to their simple meaning?

After all this, it is proper to be very astonished by [the Christians]. If the Ten Commandments exist and we are obligated to observe them, is not the Sabbath included in them, and where did they find a place to annul it and not observe it?[69] If it is said, since Sunday is for rest according to those who say it is the seventh day and the Sabbath, this is not adequate, since [the Sabbath's] true meaning is to cease from all labor on that very day.[70] It is proper that we rest on it from all our labor. Moreover, should we abandon that very day which is the day on which God, may He be blessed, rested, and take instead the day on which he started the work of creation,[71] then it is clear that the intention of resting on that day would be lost. This is the opposite of what God intended. From all of this, the refutation of that second premise follows. Moses, peace be upon him, has already said: "The secret things belong to the Lord our God; but the things that are revealed belong to us and our children for ever, that we may do all the words of this Torah."[72] This shows its total future eternity forever, as it says: "that we may do all the words of this Torah," and just as Maimonides, of blessed memory, said.[73]

III. We have now only to speak against the third premise in which they say that the Torah does not give spiritual enjoyment and does not give good to the soul.[74] We say: Even though [the Torah] does not state it clearly, when it is investigated, it can be seen already that this clearly follows. Concerning Enoch, it said, "Enoch walked with God; and he was not, for God took him."[75] Or as it said about Elijah, "Today the Lord will take away your master from over you."[76] In the matter of the binding of Isaac, it is clear also. For if [there were no spiritual reward], what did Abraham expect from the blessings which were to be fulfilled through Isaac? As for Isaac himself, who was willing to prepare for death, if he did not rely on the enjoyment of the soul after it separated from his body, what was the source of his certainty after death?[77] Circumcision itself, which, even they admit, came to ease the punishment of the soul brought about by original sin,[78] is one of the 613 commandments, and, concerning it, [Scripture] speaks of the penalty of "excision,"[79] which is the loss of the soul. It follows that one who serves God and does this will merit enjoyment, for the knowledge of opposites is one.[80] Our fathers in Egypt were certain about this even as they suffered that exile and terrible persecution from the Egyptians, for they did not become involved with them to become one nation,[81] since they knew and believed that they would merit an inestimable pleasure after death. They received [this belief] from their holy fathers Abraham, Isaac, and Jacob. How can reason permit that they would permit this suffering without certainty and belief?[82] Its well known nature led Balaam to say, "Let me die the death of the righteous, and let my end be like his."[83] He desired that after his death he be in the company of the souls of the children of Israel.[84] King David, of blessed memory, hints about this eternal life in many places in the Psalms:[85] "My portion in the land of the living";[86] "I believe that I shall see the goodness of the Lord in the land of the living";[87] he said about Doeg, "But God will break you down forever . . . He will uproot you from the land of the living forever."[88] This shows that there was something called the "Land of the Living,"[89] in which there is "life forever," and this is the world to come.[90] Because of his great sin in which he incited Saul to kill the priests of God and to pursue his anointed one, he was cut off and separated from that eternal life.[91]

It[92] is impossible that there be another interpretation because it is so clear. Just as the Rabbi, of blessed memory, wrote, "The knowledge of opposites is one," then just as the one who hates and is the enemy of God is "uprooted from the land of the living forever," so, too, does the holy worshipper inherit it, as it says, "The righteous shall see, and fear, and shall laugh at him."[93]

The prophet Isaiah said, "Israel is saved by the Lord with everlasting salvation."[94] There is no need to bring a proof other than from the Torah of Moses itself, namely, from the passage in which he called Israel "a holy nation and a kingdom of priests, My own possession among all peoples,"[95] and he said at the end of his Torah: "Happy are you, O Israel! Who is like you, a people saved by the Lord."[96] The happiness and felicity could not refer to imaginary [that is, temporary] goods, yet [this would be the case] if the soul after its separation [from the body] were to be in darkness and deep shadow.[97] In the reliable and true stories of history in the book of Joseph ben Gurion,[98] we find that there were sages and saints who suffered chastisements and strange deaths and were killed for the sanctification of the Lord, may He be blessed, because they hoped for the true reward from the Master of reward, may He be exalted. It is also possible to bring a proof that everything mentioned about punishments and physical things was of secondary intention, but the Torah's primary intention was to help them acquire eternal life,[99] as the Lord, may He be blessed, said: "If you will diligently hearken to the voice of the Lord your God, and do that which is right in His eyes, and give heed to His commandments and keep all His statutes, I will put none of the diseases upon you which I put upon the Egyptians; for I am the Lord, your healer."[100] It is not proper to think that the reward of all these things is being guarded from the Egyptian diseases! Rather, it is proper that the reward is their attainment of high stature and degree. It is clear that the imaginary goods and evils are not the primary intention but are a means and a guidance for acquiring the life of the eternal world.[101] For this reason, he said that with the observance of the commandments we shall be healthy in order to worship God and to apprehend the truth of His secrets.[102] [In this manner] people will achieve the love and fear of Him with which they will acquire "the light of the face of the King, namely, life"[103] in the unending world. All these promises were the certainty that those things which prevent felicity would be absent. For this reason, what we acquire of governance and greatness are not essential but are only so that we be free, with "neither adversary nor misfortune,"[104] to keep us from speculating and knowing God, as water covers the sea,[105] and to cleave to Him,[106] for He is our true life. This is sufficient for this chapter.

CHAPTER 10

Concerning Demons

The Christian belief is that in the first instant of [the demons'] existence, they sinned with jealousy and maliciousness.[1] As a result, even though they were angels of peace, free will was taken away from them.[2] The arguments which can be made against this opinion are, first of all, that many refutations pointing to reprehensible consequences follow from it.

I. First, if they sinned at the first instant of their existence,[3] then it follows that they never had free will at any time, because when they sinned in actuality, they did not have free will.[4] It has already been clearly explained in *Physics*, book I,[5] that there is no existence in actuality in the first instant. Therefore, they did not have free will in actuality in the first instant of their existence. Yet, before they sinned, they did not exist; and if they did not have free will, they did not sin. It is clear that sin requires free will, for he who has no free will cannot sin.[6] But it has already been posited that they sinned. This is an impossible inconsistency.

II. Second, if they sinned in the first instant and immediately free will was removed from them, it necessarily follows that it was removed from them either in the very same instant in which they sinned or after they sinned. Now, it is impossible that free will was taken from them some time after they sinned, for then they would exist with free will for some time after they sinned, unless you say free will was taken from them in the instant after they sinned. But then one instant would come after another and instants would conjoin with each other without any time between them.[7] As a result, it follows that if free will were removed from them after they sinned, then there was some time in which they existed with their free will. Since time is infinitely divisible, all of which has been clearly explained in *Physics*, book VI,[8] it follows that when they were punished by having free will taken away, it was already proper that they be punished, that is, they had already remained in their high stature some time after they had sinned, namely, the time in which they still had free will. It is a reprehensible consequence of their position that the angels would have been worthy of punishment before they were punished or that they remained[9] after their sin for a period of time with their high stature, namely, free will, for they say that the punishment is the removal of free will from them as a result of their evil. It follows, then, that at the very same instant in which they sinned, free will was removed from them. Now, you have already said that they sinned at the very first instant. Therefore, at that instant they must have had free will. It follows that in the very same instant they had free will, and they did not have free will. This is a great contradiction.[10]

It is proper that you know that they are required to accept all these refutations, because if the angels did not sin at the beginning of their existence and had existed for some time with their high stature and free will, they would not have sinned. Therefore, according to their opinion, they would have been maintained by divine grace, as, according to their opinion,[11] the other [angels] are maintained, and, as a result, they would not have sinned. But it follows that they did sin at the first instant and, so, all the refutations which you have already seen will catch up with them. It is clear, however, that one cannot think to attribute sin to the nature of the separate [intellects] since sin, disrespect, and deficiency in things comes from their matter, whereas perfection and stature come from form, as has been clearly explained in *Metaphysics*.[12] Since the nature of angels is intelligent form, it is absolutely impossible for them in their nature to choose evil. When we say about them that they have free will, we mean that there is an inclination to do good and to love both truth and the Agent of perfection. In this manner, the terms "will" and "free will" can be used in reference to separate [intellects], not that they really have the possibility or choice of doing evil. That is absolutely impossible for separate intellects.[13] If it were possible for them by their nature to choose evil, it would have to be for some purpose and end, and, therefore, it would follow that the agent [namely, the angels] would temporally precede his action, as is the case with any purposeful and willful agent which precedes his action. As a result, they could not have sinned in that first instant in which they existed.[14] This is the opposite of what has been posited. It follows from this that if they did not sin at the very first instant, since time must precede the sin, then it is proper that at that time in which they did not sin, they were maintained by grace, just as the other angels of high stature were maintained. What follows from all this is that the demons were never good angels. That is sufficient for this chapter.

Joseph said: But their speculation forced them to say that the demons were good angels who sinned with their evil free will, since their existence is clearly found in the Torah: "They sacrificed to demons [*shedim*] which were no gods;"[15] "so they shall no more slay their sacrifices for satyrs [*se'irim*]."[16] It is even clearer in their Torah since Satan wished to test

Jesus,[17] and the latter healed many people who had demons in them.[18] It is almost the case that this opinion, namely, the existence of demons, is widely publicized and accepted in all the nations. Since the [Christians] thought that it is impossible that something evil can come from God, they needed to say that the [demons] were created good but they themselves became wicked. The [Christians] fell into those contradictions which you have seen.

This rabbi, of blessed memory, accepted these two premises in his book *Light of the Lord*,[19] in which he accepted the existence of demons as he did here, while most philosophers denied their existence.[20]

Maimonides, of blessed memory, explained the statement "They sacrificed to demons [*shedim*] which were no gods"[21] as referring to imaginary, nonexisting things. He adduced the statement of the sages, of blessed memory, in Sifre: "It is not enough that they worship the sun, the moon, the stars and the constellations, but they even worship their imagination."[22] He said that [the sages] of blessed memory meant that they continued worshipping existing things until they started worshipping imaginary things, hinting, thereby, that [the demons] do not exist.[23] Likewise in three places in his book he hinted at this.[24] But the simple meaning of the Scriptures and most of the words of the sages[25] establish their existence without doubt, and this is a very well publicized opinion.

As to their quiddity, this rabbi in his book *Light of the Lord*[26] has already spoken and solved the difficulty which had caused the Christians to maintain that they were of high stature. [He did this with] that indubitably reasonable premise, namely that no essential evil descends from above, but [evil] does follow by accident or by second intention, since matter and privation exist, as Maimonides, of blessed memory, expounded at length in part III.[27] This rabbi, of blessed memory, said, however, that God intended their existence to be hidden from man for the purpose of testing, rewarding, and punishing, which is good, thereby agreeing with the premise.[28] But if, indeed, every existent was intended for its own essence, as Maimonides clearly explained in part III, chapter 13, in that incomparably recondite and marvelous way, then, if they were essentially bad and sinful (as would follow from their nature), a doubt would arise. If they have desire and free will, it is possible that they will want the good, and if a possibility is posited to exist, this presupposition cannot be annulled. But their existence *is* essentially not good, and their free will *is* annulled, as is posited and told about them. Maybe some of them are good as is told in some of the Aggadot. Then, why are demons called spoilers[29] and Satans? Maybe they have different species. Maybe their free will always inclines toward evil, just as the free will of separate intellects is toward good. Therefore, the question remains: How could a bad thing come from God Who is the absolute good?

I saw that some Kabbalists[30] posited that among the separate things, there are powers of impurity. This rabbi, of blessed memory, wished to refute this opinion by stating that good comes from their form and evil from their matter. I am amazed! If they are intelligent, composite beings, as this rabbi, of blessed memory, posited, then one could justifiably say that they are rational, mortal animals, and, therefore, they are of the human species. This must be the case unless we posit that "rational animal" can be divided into "man" and "demon," just as "nonrational animal" is the genus of the animal species. Oh, that I knew[31] if he used "rationality" univocally or equivocally or amphibolously.[32] How can they be seen and how can they disappear from humans if they wear dense, terrestrial bodies in animal or other shapes? How can the demon become corporeal, and how are the elements composed in it, and what humors are in it? How will they posit it: If it has form, is it connected with it as a body is connected with another body? Maybe these things are according to the thoughts of those who see them, and they have no existence outside the intellect? In general, one who has learned physics and understands how bodies are generated and the quality of their composition, and one who knows the secrets of the existents and the truth of form in metaphysics, and the agent and the final cause, will find[33] great perplexities and enormous doubts in this investigation, and it is possible that the issue is not subject to demonstrative proof. Whatever the case, since those who hold this view are the group of sages of our Torah, the Kabbalists,[34] one may not move even a hairbreadth from their tradition even if they say to you that right is left.[35] If it is tradition we shall accept it happily.[36] We shall turn apparently decisive arguments into doubts and try to resolve them. This brief format does not allow this [here].[37] We return to the words of the book. He said:

I think that I have concluded what I intended to do in this treatise as was set forth in my introduction.

Here is completed what I have seen proper to translate from these chapters, and these are things which are fully revealed and publicized with the help of my explanatory elaborations. When one adds to this treatise my comments on the *Epistle* of En Profiat, then anyone into whose hands these two treatises fall can, with the help of God, give a true answer[38] [to the Christians] and send them away empty-handed with respect to the wisdom and speculation in them.

I had found another treatise of this rabbi, of blessed memory, written in the vernacular, in which he responded to those arguments taken from the prophets which [the Christians] had made to maintain their belief.[39] Yet I was too lazy to translate it since there are very many of this kind in our nation, as I mentioned in the introduction to my *Commentary on the Epistle* of En Profiat,[40] and I was occupied at that time with other matters, serving these kings.[41] Nevertheless, because of my love of truth and its advocates, I made an effort to find some free time [to translate this work], which I did here in Alcala de Henares[42] in the last ten days of Av, 5211.[43] May God grant me and all Israel who are friends the merit to place our lot among the righteous who will see and rejoice, the upright who will exalt, and the pious who will thrill with delight, and may iniquity shut its mouth and all wickedness vanish like smoke,[44] "for the earth shall be as full with the knowledge of the Lord as the water covers the sea."[45] May God, who has helped us, be blessed and raised above all blessing and praise. Amen. Amen. Selah. Va‘ed.[46]

NOTES

FOREWORD TO THE ENGLISH TRANSLATION

1. A general overview of the period is provided by Yitzhaq (Fritz) Baer, *A History of the Jews in Christian Spain*, Philadelphia, 1971, vol. 2, pp. 95 – 299.

2. See *ibid.*, p. 523 (index, s.v. Hasdai Crescas).

3. See *Or Adonai (Light of the Lord)*, Vienna, 1859 (reprinted, no place, no date). Concerning this work, see especially Harry A. Wolfson, *Crescas' Critique of Aristotle*, Cambridge, Mass., 1929.

4. Joseph ben Shem Tov refers to the vernacular as *"leshon arₓo"* (the language of his land). As to which language that is, see below.

Crescas also wrote a Sermon for Passover; see Aviezer Ravitsky, *Crescas' Sermon on the Passover and Studies in His Philosophy*, Jerusalem, 1988 (in Hebrew; this work appeared too late for me to make use of it in preparation of the translation of Crescas' *Refutation*).

5. Our only source of the existence of this work is Joseph ben Shem Tov's comments at the end of his translation of *The Refutation*; see Chapter 10. The distinctions among exegetical, historical, and philosophical arguments are discussed in my *Jewish Philosophical Polemics Against Christianity in the Middle Ages*, New York, 1977, pp. 1 – 12.

6. Joseph ben Shem Tov wrote, "I was too lazy to translate it since there are very many of this kind in our nation, as I explained in the introduction to my *Commentary on the Epistle* of En Profiat [see next note], and I was occupied at that time with other matters, serving these kings."

The version of the Disputation of Tortosa preserved in Solomon Ibn Verga's *Shevet Yehudah* (ed. A. Shochat and Y. Baer, Jerusalem, 1947, p. 103), refers to Crescas' opinion concerning the birth of the messiah. This opinion is not mentioned in any of Crescas' extant works, and, so, it is possible that it is taken from this other polemical treatise.

7. We have no idea whence Crescas derived this list or what he meant by listing these beliefs as root principles. In *Light of the Lord*, Crescas offered an original formulation of Jewish principles, dividing them into roots (*shorashim:* beliefs which serve as the presupposition of revelation), cornerstones (*pinnot:* beliefs which make revelation possible), and true beliefs (*emunot amittiyyot:* beliefs actually taught by the Torah of Moses). In general, Crescas saw all these doctrines as beliefs which must be accepted by people claiming to believe in the Torah of Moses if they wish to avoid self-contradiction. This account of the principles of Judaism is quite different from Maimonides' view that the dogmas of Judaism are those beliefs which lead to personal salvation. See Menachem Kellner, *Dogma in Medieval Jewish Thought*, Oxford, 1986, pp. 108 – 139.

In his *Commentary* on Profiat Duran's *Iggeret Al Tehi Ka-'Avotekha (Epistle Be Not Like Your Fathers)*, Joseph ben Shem Tov wrote that Crescas' polemic was an example of "the method of one who intended to raise objections against every one of the principles of belief, called roots *articulos* [the Castilian term appears in Hebrew letters]"; see Joseph ben Shem Tov, *Commentary on the Epistle Be Not Like Your Fathers*, in the edition of Duran's *Epistle*, published by the Akademon, Hebrew University, Jerusalem, 1969/70, on the basis of the Adolf (Zev) Poznanski manuscript, Jewish National and University Library ms. Heb 8° 757, p. 24. We do not know whether the Castilian term *articulos* is Crescas' or Joseph's.

In Profiat Duran's *Disgrace of the Gentiles*, most of the topics discussed here are mentioned, but they appear in a different order and are not classified as principles of faith.

8. On Joseph ben Shem Tov, see Shaul Regev, *Theology and Rational Mysticism in the Writings of R. Joseph ben Shem Tov*, Hebrew University dissertation, June 1983 (in Hebrew).

9. Both in this work and in Joseph's *Commentary on the Epistle,* p. 26.

10. See Ben-Zion Netanyahu, *The Marranos of Spain,* New York, 1966, p. 87, n. 11; Frank Talmage, *The Polemical Writings of Profiat Duran,* Jerusalem, 1981, p. 14 (in editor's introduction).

11. I.e., "treatise" in Castilian; see, e.g., Netanyahu, *Marranos,* p. 221.

12. Johannes Bern. De-Rossi, *Bibliotheca Judaica Antichristiana,* Parma, 1800 (reprinted, Amsterdam, 1969), pp. 24 – 25, 39 – 41.

13. "Ma'amar asher ʿasah bi-leshon arẓo bi-sefeiqot emunat ha-'umah ha-Noẓrit"; see Abravanel, *Shamayim Ḥadashim,* Roedelheim, 1828 (reprinted, Jerusalem, 1966/67), p. 28a. See also Abravanel's *Commentary* to Isaiah 52 in *Peirush ʿAl Nevi'im Aḥaronim,* Jerusalem, 1955/56, p. 242.

14. *The Separate Treatise* (?); see Moritz Steinschneider, *Catalogus Librorum Hebraeorum,* Berlin, 1852 – 1860 (reprinted, Hildesheim, 1964), cols. 1529 – 1530. Steinschneider knew the name *Refutation of the Christian Principles* from Breslau ms. 59, but thought that that was not the correct name of the work; see his *Catalogus Codicum Hebraeorum Bibliothecae Academiae Lugduno-Batavae,* Leiden, 1858, pp. 277 – 278.

15. De-Rossi, *Bibliotheca,* pp. 24 – 25, 39 – 41.

16. For the variants of the manuscripts, see my Hebrew edition: Daniel J. Lasker, *Hasdai Crescas' Bittul Iqqarei Ha-Noẓrim,* Ramat-Gan and Beer Sheva, 1990, pp. 23 – 27.

17. See below, Chapter 8; Netanyahu, *Marranos,* pp. 221 – 223; Wolfson, *Crescas',* pp. 16 – 18. Apparently, Crescas wrote *Light of the Lord* in stages, and it is possible that parts of the philosophical work were completed before the writing of *The Refutation of the Christian Principles.*

18. *Commentary on the Epistle,* pp. 24 – 26.

19. These expressions are found in Chapters 1, 2, 4, 6. For a similar methodology, see *Light of the Lord,* p. 20a.

20. See Crescas' Preface.

21. Other polemicists of the same period were Shem Tov Ibn Shaprut, and Moses Ha-Cohen of Tordesillas (both fourteenth century), and Simeon ben Zemah Duran and Joseph Albo (both fifteenth century). The ideology of the philosophical polemicists is discussed in Lasker, *Polemics*, 25 – 43; and *idem*, "Averroistic Trends in Jewish-Christian Polemics in the Late Middle Ages," *Speculum*, 55:2 (1980): 294 – 304.

22. Both works are edited in Talmage, *Polemical Writings.*

23. *Ibid.,* p. 14 (introduction).

24. *Ibid.,* pp. 16, 34.

25. Netanyahu, *Marranos*, pp. 86 – 87, sees the commissioning of *The Disgrace* by Crescas as part of a campaign against converts to Christianity. Since, however, the book did not meet his needs, he wrote *The Refutation.*

26. In Talmage, *Polemical Writings,* pp. 17 – 18.

27. Chapters 1, 2, and 9 (and notes). See also my article, "Original Sin and Its Atonement According to Hasdai Crescas," *Daat*, 20 (Winter 1988): 127 – 135 (in Hebrew).

28. Shalom Rosenberg, "The *Arba'ah Turim* of Rabbi Abraham bar Judah, Disciple of Don Hasdai Crescas," *Jerusalem Studies in Jewish Thought*, 3:4 (1983/84), pp. 525, 596 – 97 (in Hebrew).

29. See Crescas' Preface.

30. Heinrich Graetz, *History of the Jews*, Philadelphia, 1894, vol 4., p. 187. A number of other writers have followed Graetz and have written that Crescas wrote his book for non-Jews; see, e.g., Ephraim E. Urbach, *"Apologetiqah," Encyclopaedia Hebraica*, vol. 5, Jerusalem-Tel Aviv, 1952/53, col. 131.

31. Netanyahu, *Marranos*, pp. 86 – 87. According to his opinion, Crescas' campaign to prevent apostasy "clearly shows that by 1397, only six years after the great conversion, there was already afoot, among the forced converts, a strong movement toward real

Christianization which threatened to dominate that camp." See also Israel Zinberg, *A History of Jewish Literature*, vol. 3, Cleveland and London, 1973, p. 203, n. 28.

32. Even Joseph ben Shem Tov had problems sometimes understanding the original; see Chapter 3. Netanyahu's remark (*Marranos*, p. 86) that Crescas' intention in writing *The Refutation of the Christian Principles* was to present "a less scholarly work" than Duran's *Disgrace* is somewhat surprising.

33. There was no dearth of polemical works written in Hebrew, especially those dealing with prophetical proof-texts.

Moses Ha-Kohen of Tordesillas also wrote an anti-Christian philosophical polemic in the vernacular because of the difficulties his Jewish audience would have in understanding a Hebrew treatise; see Yehuda Shamir, *Rabbi Moses Ha-Kohen of Tordesillas and his Book 'Ezer Ha-Emunah — A Chapter in the History of the Judeo-Christian Controversy*, Coconut Grove, Fla., 1972, vol. 2, p. 174.

34. It is possible that Joseph ben Shem Tov's students specifically had difficulty with Crescas' vernacular since they lived in Castile. Nevertheless, Joseph wrote that they could read compositions only in Hebrew and that their knowledge of philosophy was weak; see Joseph ben Shem Tov's Introduction. Don Isaac Abravanel (approximately one hundred years after Crescas) knew only Joseph ben Shem Tov's translation, and it is possible that by then the original was already lost; see Abravanel, *Shamayim Hadashim*, p. 28a.

35. See Joseph ben Shem Tov's Introduction.

36. See also Joseph's comments in *Commentary on the Epistle*, p. 26, in which he said that he would have liked to have written a second commentary on Duran's work.

37. See Chapter 10, end.

38. See notes to Chapter 4.

39. See the end of the translation.

40. See, e.g., the end of Chapter 9.

41. See the end of Chapter 3.

42. See the middle of Chapter 3.

43. See Chapter 1.

44. Chapter 1; see also my article "Original Sin."

45. See Chapters 3, 6, 10. The contradiction is, in fact, blatant only in Chapter 6; see notes to Chapter 6.

46. Cf. *Light of the Lord* II, 6, with *The Refutation of the Christian Principles*, Chapter 9.

47. I have attempted in the notes to point out both the contradictions and the points of contact between the two works.

48. See Wolfson, *Crescas*', pp. 16 – 18, also see n. 17. Abravanel adopted Joseph ben Shem Tov's explanation, and he argued that Crescas' change of mind came about as a result of his having read Al-Ghazali's *The Incoherence of the Philosophers* and Averroes' *The Incoherence of the Incoherence;* see Abravanel, *Shamayim Hadashim*, p. 28a.

49. Rosenberg, *Arbaʿah Turim*, p. 527.

50. *Ibid.;* for a theory of development in Crescas' thought in another area, see Aviezer Ravitsky, "Crescas' Theory on Human Will: Development and Sources," *Tarbiz*, 51 (1981/82): 445 – 469 (in Hebrew). The thesis of this article was developed further in Ravitsky's edition of the *Sermon on the Passover*.

51. See Lasker, *Polemics*, pp. 87 – 89; 165 – 167. If the original intended readers of Crescas's polemic were educated, assimilated Jews who had accepted the views of Aristotle, it is possible that Crescas phrased his arguments specifically in light of their beliefs.

52. See n. 16.

53. Crescas knew Christian philosophical sources; see Shlomo Pines, "Scholasticism after Thomas Aquinas and the Teachings of Hasdai Crescas and his Predecessors," *Proceedings of the Israel Academy of Sciences and Humanities,* I, 10, Jerusalem, 1967; Ravitsky, "Crescas' Theory." Seymour Feldman doubts that Crescas' theory of determinism depended on Christian thinkers; see his "Crescas' Theological Determinism," *Daat*, 9 (Summer 1982): 11 – 12.

JOSEPH BEN SHEM TOV'S INTRODUCTION

1. Ps. 119:98; for the manuscript variants of the first line, see my Hebrew edition.

2. Deut. 4:20.

3. Ex. 19:6.

4. Song of Songs 3:8; the reference here is not to military warfare.

5. From the prayer *u-va' le-ẓiyyon go'el.*

6. From the prayer *'Aleinu le-shabe-aḥ.*

7. Cf. Prov. 13:5.

8. In other words, the Christians deny both the senses and reason. This idea is taken from Profiat Duran (Isaac ben Moses Halevi, "Efodi"), *Epistle Be Not Like Your Fathers (Iggeret Al Tehi Ka-'Avotekha),* in Frank Talmage, *The Polemical Writings of Profiat Duran,* Jerusalem, 1981, pp. 76 – 78. See also Duran, *The Disgrace of the Gentiles (Sefer Kelimmat Ha-Goyim),* in *ibid.,* p. 37.

9. Cf. Is. 38:19.

10. From the prayer *'Aleinu le-shabe-ah*; cf. Is. 45:20.

11. Ps. 100:3.

12. From the prayer *'Aleinu le-shabe-aḥ.*

13. Is. 63:1.

14. Cf. Ex. 15:17.

15. Ez. 28:2.

16. I Chron. 29:11.

17. Cf. Neh. 9:5.

18. Obad. 1:20. For the use of this verse to prove the ancient roots of the Jewish community in Spain (Sepharad), see Yitzhak Baer, *A History of the Jews in Christian Spain,* Philadelphia, 1971, vol. 1, p. 16; see also Duran, *Disgrace,* p. 3.

19. Cf. Jer. 51:34. Ben-Zion Netanyahu identified the "en-

emies" here with Jewish converts to Christianity; see his *The Marranos of Spain*, New York, 1966, pp. 93 – 94.

20. From the Haggadah of Passover.

21. Cf. Ps. 12:4.

22. Jer. 16:19. This verse was a central motif in the Jewish-Christian debate; see, e.g., Duran, *Epistle*, p. 73; Maimonides, *Mishneh Torah*, "Laws of Kings," 11, 4 (in uncensored editions); L. Landau, *Das Apologetische Schreiben des Josua Lorki*, Antwerp, 1906, p. 1. See Crescas' usage of the verse in *Light of the Lord*, Vienna, 1859 (reprinted, n.p. and n.d.), III, 4, 2, p. 76a. For the importance of learning from one's parents and habit as sources of error, see Daniel J. Lasker, *Jewish Philosophical Polemics Against Christianity in the Middle Ages*, New York, 1977, pp. 25 – 27.

23. Cf. Esther 7:5.

24. Cf. Ps. 51:14.

25. Ps. 137:7

26. Joseph ben Shem Tov's *Commentary on the Epistle Be Not Like Your Fathers* of Profiat Duran is found in the edition of *Epistle* published by the Akademon, Hebrew University, Jerusalem, 1969/70, which is based on the Adolf (Zev) Poznanski manuscript, Jewish National and University Library, ms. Heb 8⁰ 757. The title *En* in Catalan is equivalent to *Don* in Castilian; see Talmage, *Polemical Writings*, p. 9 (introduction).

27. See *Commentary on the Epistle*, pp. 22 – 26; Lasker, *Polemics*, Chapter 2.

28. *Commentary on the Epistle*, pp. 24 – 26.

29. It is unclear to which vernacular language Joseph ben Shem Tov referred; see the Foreword to the English Translation.

30. Cf. Is. 29:11. For a similar usage, see Duran, *Epistle*, p. 73.

31. Job 29:3.

32. Cf. Ps. 111:6.

33. The reference may be to the results of the mass conversions in Spain.

34. II Kings 17:26, 27.

35. Speculation, Hebrew *'iyyun*, refers to philosophical investigations.

36. Cf. Gen. 41:39.

37. Hebrew *moreh ẓedeq;* cf. Joel 2:23 (*moreh li-ẓedaqah,* abundant rain).

38. Cf. Jer. 10:10.

39. Hosea 2:1.

40. Ps. 149:6.

41. Cf. Prov. 22:21.

42. Cf. Dan. 1:4.

43. This is, therefore, the second edition of the translation by Joseph ben Shem Tov; see the Foreword to the English Translation.

44. Cf. Deut. 31:21.

45. This Hebrew translation is intended, therefore, to serve as a guide to Jewish polemicists with Christianity, providing them with a "double-edged sword" to fight "an obligatory war" (*milḥemet miẓvah*) against conversion.

46. Gen. 4:14. See Shaul Regev, *Theology and Rational Mysticism in the Writings of R. Joseph ben Shem Tov,* Hebrew University dissertation, 1983, p. 7.

47. From the prayer *'Aleinu le-shabe-aḥ.*

48. Cf. Is. 66:23.

49. Is. 11:9.

50. For Joseph ben Shem Tov's method of translation, see the Foreword to the English Translation.

51. I.e., Hasdai Crescas.

HASDAI CRESCAS' PREFACE

1. There is a disagreement as to whether the reference is to Jewish or to non-Jewish nobles. It is more reasonable to assume that Crescas was referring to Jews; see the Foreword to the English Translation.

2. First one must give a conception (*ziyyur*) of the belief before its verification (*immut*). Hence, Crescas first presented the principles, and the premises on which they are based, and only afterward analyzed them. *Ziyyur* and *immut* are mentioned together by Crescas in *Light of the Lord*, p. 54b. For the background of these terms, see Harry A. Wolfson, "The Terms *Tasawwur* and *Tasdiq* in Arabic Philosophy and Their Greek, Latin and Hebrew Equivalents," *The Moslem World*, 33 (1943): 1–15 (reprinted in *Studies in the History of Philosophy and Religion*, vol. 1, Cambridge, Mass, 1973, pp. 478–492).

3. Cf. Is. 58:4.

4. We do not know the source of Crescas' list of Christian principles, nor his meaning in calling them principles; see the Foreword to the English Translation.

5. Hebrew *zevihat mizbaham*, literally, "the sacrifice of their altar."

6. Above, this principle is referred to as "the original universal sin of Adam"; at the beginning of Chapter 1, it is called "the punishment of Adam's sin."

7. According to Thomas Aquinas, the physical punishment was the entrance of death into the world; see *Summa Theologiae (Summa)*, I, 97,1; II–II, 164, 1 (following Rom. 5:12). In *Summa*, II–II, 164, 2, Thomas dealt with other physical punishments. For Jewish beliefs concerning the introduction of sin into the world, see B. Shab. 55a–b; Frederick R. Tennant, *The Sources of the Doctrine of the Fall and Original Sin*, New York, 1968; Samuel S. Cohon, "Original Sin," *Hebrew Union College Annual*, 21 (1948): 275–330.

8. This premise is also the first premise of the second principle.

9. Literally, "the Garden of Eden."

10. See Thomas, *Summa*, I – II, 85, 5.

11. Yet, see the second premise of the second principle. The idea of an original sin passed on by inheritance from Adam to all his descendants is not entirely absent from the Jewish tradition, and even Crescas himself held a certain view of original sin in his *Light of the Lord*. See Chapter 1, notes.

12. In Chapter 2, this principle is called "redemption from Adam's original sin called in their language 'original'."

13. In Chapter 3, the order is slightly different (i.e., 4, 3, 6, 5). For the Christian sources, see the notes there.

14. Hebrew *mahut*, the "whatness" or essence of something.

15. Hebrew *ma'alot*, literally degrees, virtues.

16. Literally; "in his language, *Personas*."

17. For the Christian sources, see notes to Chapter 4.

18. Hebrew *beten*, literally, "belly", used for both stomach and womb.

19. For the Christian sources, see notes to Chapter 5.

20. See n. 5.

21. Hebrew *'ugah*, in its original meaning of thin bread; see Gen. 18:6 and Ex. 12:39.

22. In other words, the elements of the Eucharist do not become merely part of the incarnate Son, but the whole Son, in terms both of quantity and glory.
There is no description of the Christian doctrine in Chapter 6. Cf. the description here with that of Duran, *Disgrace*, pp. 35 – 36; and see also Lasker, *Polemics*, pp. 136 – 137. Thomas dealt with this Christian sacrament in *Summa*, III, 73 – 83.

23. There is no description of this Christian doctrine in Chapter 7. See, e.g., Thomas, *Summa Contra Gentiles [SCG]*, IV, 50: "Baptismus infantibus datur ut . . . ad regnum Dei perveniri,

quo perveniant non potest sine baptismo." Crescas borrowed the Jewish expression "has no place in the world to come" from M. Sanh. 10:1.

24. The order in Chapter 9 is different than that here; for the Christian sources, see notes there.

25. E.g., the Ten Commandments.

26. Hebrew *ḥuqqim*, i.e., laws for which there are no reasons.

27. For the Christian sources, see the notes to Chapter 10.

28. I.e., the rational axioms.

29. These two premises are the basis of the Jewish philosophical polemics against Christianity in the fourteenth and fifteenth centuries; see Lasker, *Polemics*, chapter 3; *idem*, "Averroistic Trends in Jewish-Christian Polemics in the Late Middle Ages," *Speculum*, 55:2 (1980): 294 – 304. Christian philosophers generally agreed with these two premises; see, e.g., Thomas, *SCG*, I, 7; II, 25. Crescas' use here of these propositions is not merely polemical, since he expressed a similar opinion in *Light of the Lord*, II, 3, I, p. 40b (on God's power); III, 4, 4, p.76b. See also the Foreword to the English Translation.

30. See Saadia Gaon, *Book of Beliefs and Opinions*, IV. Christians also generally agreed with this premise; see Thomas, *Summa*, I, 22, 1; Anselm of Canterbury, *Cur Deus Homo*, II, 1, *Opera Omnia*, Stuttgart-Bad-Canstatt, 1968, vol. 2, pp. 97 – 98.

31. Deut. 6:24.

32. Hebrew *ḥazaqah*, i.e., a legal right based on possession.

33. Although this looks like a last line of defense, Crescas may be expressing here the idea that the later religions which were imitating the original divine religion are necessarily false; cf. Maimonides, *Guide*, II, 40. Crescas may also be reflecting the Averroistic notion that philosophy is not sufficient to determine the relative truth of religions; see my "Averroistic Trends."

CHAPTER 1
CONCERNING THE PUNISHMENT OF ADAM'S SIN

1. Literally, "concerning punishment of the sin of the first man" ("*adam ha-rishon*"). Crescas did not completely reject the concept of original sin; it features in his work *Light of the Lord* (see II, 2, 6; pp. 38b – 39a). See also my "Original Sin and Its Atonement According to Hasdai Crescas," *Daat*, 20 (Winter 1988): 127 – 135 (in Hebrew). For a general review of Jewish arguments against the Christian doctrine of original sin, see Joel E. Rembaum, "Medieval Jewish Criticism of the Christian Doctrine of Original Sin," *AJS Review*, 7 – 8 (1982 – 83): 353 – 382.

2. Thomas, *Summa*, II – II, 163, 3.

3. *Ibid.*, I, 95, 3.

4. *Ibid.*, 1.

5. *Ibid.*, 3.

6. See Rom. 5:12, 17; *Summa*, II – II, 164, 1, ad 3.

7. *Ibid.*, I – II, 79, 3; 85, 5; 98, 4, ad 3.

8. Hebrew *'avodot*, e.g., divine service, obedience to commandments.

9. Hebrew *ḥakhmei ha-tei'ologiah*. One of the principles of Christianity holds that eternal life cannot be achieved through the commandments; it is a result solely of the acceptance of Jesus as the messiah and through divine grace; see Rom. 1 – 8; Gal. 2:21; Thomas, *Summa*, I – II, 112, 1; 114, 2. Thomas maintained that someone who observed the commandments after the coming of Jesus was in violation of a moral commandment (*ibid.*, 103, 4).

10. For another Jewish description of original sin, see Duran, *Disgrace*, pp. 17 – 23. Thomas dealt with the objections to the Christian doctrine, and possible solutions to them, in *SCG*, IV, 51 – 52.

11. Hebrew *'iyyun;* see Joseph ben Shem Tov's Introduction, n. 35.

12. Literally, the Garden of Eden.

13. Hebrew *'avodah*.

14. In *Light of the Lord*, Crescas objected strenuously to the view that permanence of the soul is dependent on intellectual achievements rather than on observance of the commandments; see Warren (Zeev) Harvey, *Hasdai Crescas's Critique of the Theory of the Acquired Intellect*, Columbia University dissertation, 1973; *idem*, "Crescas versus Maimonides on Knowledge and Pleasure," in Ruth-Link Salinger, ed., *A Straight Path. Studies in Medieval Philosophy and Culture: Essays in Honor of Arthur Hyman*, Washington, D.C., 1988, pp. 113 – 123. In Chapter 9, Crescas argued that observance of the commandments is the cause of eternal life. See also Shalom Rosenberg, "The *Arba'ah Turim* of Rabbi Abraham bar Judah, Disciple of Don Hasdai Crescas," *Jerusalem Studies in Jewish Thought*, 3:4 (1983/84): 582 (in Hebrew).

15. Some manuscripts read: "to a comfortable soul" (*le-nefesh no-ah lo*). Crescas refers to Noah in the next paragraph and in *Light of the Lord*, p. 37a.

16. See, e.g., *Summa*, I, 118, 3. It is possible that Crescas believed in reincarnation; see *Light of the Lord*, IV, 7, p. 89b; Warren (Zeev) Harvey, "Kabbalistic Elements in Crescas' Light of the Lord," *Jerusalem Studies in Jewish Thought*, II:1 (1982/83): 101 – 103 (in Hebrew).

17. See Harvey, *Critique*, p. 142.

18. Cf. Ps. 51:7.

19. *Ibid.*

20. See also Thomas, *Summa*, I, 95, 4.

21. This is the third general premise posited in Crescas' Preface.

22. Cf. Ps. 89:50.

23. Literally, Garden of Eden.

24. See *Light of the Lord*, IV, 9, p. 90a; Sara Klein-Braslavy, "*Gan Eden* et *Gehinnom* dans le système de Hasdaï Crescas," in G. Nahon and C. Touati, eds., *Hommage à Georges Vajda*, Louvain, 1980, pp. 263 – 278.

25. Cf. Job 20:26.

26. For Crescas's view of permanence of the soul, see n. 14.

27. Cf. Gen. 18:25.

28. Many Christian thinkers, beginning apparently with Augustine, *De Civitate Dei* 16, 27, and other places, agreed that Jews were commanded to observe circumcision before the coming of Jesus as a partial atonement for original sin. Thomas, for instance, said (*Summa*, III, 37, 1) that circumcision comes "in remedium originalis peccati" ; cf. *ibid.*, 70; 38, 3. Crescas, in *Light of the Lord*, saw circumcision as the way of overcoming the effects of original sin; see *Light*, introduction, p. 1a; II, 2, 6, pp. 38b – 39a; III, 3, 3, p. 74a; IV, 8, p. 90a; Lasker, "Original Sin."

29. Cf. Lev. 10:18; *Summa*, III, 52, 5. In other words, according to the Christians, because of his circumcision Abraham escaped the punishments of Hell but did not merit the rewards of paradise.

30. Makkot 23b; see Ephraim E. Urbach, *The Sages — Their Concepts and Beliefs*, Jerusalem, 1975, vol. 1, pp. 342 – 365.

31. In other words, if one commandment saved Abraham from hell, then 613 commandments could certainly cause those who observe them to attain paradise.

32. Ex. 33:11.

33. Num. 12:8.

34. See Maimonides, *Commentary on the Mishnah*, "Introduction to Chapter Ḥeleq," Seventh Principle; *Mishneh Torah*, "Foundations of the Torah," 7:6; Crescas, *Light of the Lord*, III, 6, 2, pp. 79a – 80a.

CHAPTER 2
CONCERNING THE REDEMPTION FROM ADAM'S ORIGINAL SIN
CALLED IN THEIR LANGUAGE "ORIGINAL"

1. At the beginning of Chapter 1.

2. Cf. the Christian description of salvation from original sin in Anselm of Canterbury, *Cur Deus Homo*, pp. 37 – 133; see also Thomas, *Summa*, III, 1. Another Jewish account of this Christian belief can be found in Duran, *Disgrace*, pp. 17 – 18; and see also Lasker, *Polemics*, pp. 106 – 108.

3. Whereas Maimonides, *Guide*, I, 52, rejected relational attributes, Crescas argued against him on this point; see *Light of the Lord*, I, 3, 3; Harry A. Wolfson, "Crescas on the Problem of Divine Attributes," *Jewish Quarterly Review*, n.s. 7 (1916): 177 – 182 (reprinted, *Studies in the History of Philosophy and Religion*, vol. 2, Cambridge, Mass., and London, 1978, pp. 293 – 298). Thomas agreed that there is no relation between God and His creatures; see *SCG*, IV, 53.

4. I.e., in the world to come.

5. Crescas placed great value on circumcision's property of atoning for original sin; see Chapter 1, n. 28. In Duran's description of the Christian doctrine of incarnation (*Disgrace*, p. 17), he stated that according to the Christian belief even one drop of the messiah's blood was sufficient to redeem mankind. In that context, Duran made no mention of the circumcision of the messiah (though a few lines later he argued that, according to the Christians, Abraham's circumcision saved him from the punishment of Hell). The emphasis on the importance of circumcision in polemical writings of this period demonstrates the strong debate on this subject.

6. For the Christian background of this argument, see Rom. 5:19; Thomas, *Summa*, III, 48 – 49.

7. *Ibid.*, III, 48, 5; *SCG*, IV, 54.

8. Hebrew *'avodah*, see Chapter 1, n. 13.

9. The logical argument is as follows: A redeemer (in this case Jesus) must give something in order to redeem, and that

which is given for redemption must be proportional to the need of redemption. Therefore, (1) in the case of sin, redemption must come by means of worship or justice in order to be proportional, (2) this redemption, however, was not by means of worship or justice, therefore, (3) this redemption was not proportional. Crescas's intention here is to show that (2) is true (because Jesus' death was neither worship nor justice), and, hence, the Christian doctrine that the redemption was proportional is false.

10. Hebrew *setirat ha-nimshakh*.

11. Apparently, the reference is to *Nicomachean Ethics*, III, 1, even though all the manuscripts read "the first [book]".

12. Thomas, *Summa*, I – II, 6.

13. Christians argued that Jesus's death was, indeed, voluntary; see Petrus Alphonsus, *Dialogus*, X, in Jacques P. Migne, ed., *Patrologiae Cursus Completus...Series Latina [PL]*, 221 vols., Paris, 1844 – 66, 157:639 – 650; Thomas, *Summa*, III, 37, 1, ad 3.

14. Cf. Ps. 51:7.

15. Literally "that Reuben be punished for the sin of Simeon."

16. See Thomas, *SCG*, IV, 53.

17. According to the Christians, Jesus was fully human (as well as fully divine); see Thomas, *Summa*, III, 4, 6.

18. Cf. Is. 52:13. The Christians understood this verse, concerning the servant of the Lord, as referring to Jesus; see A. D. Neubauer and S. R. Driver, *The Fifty-Third Chapter of Isaiah According to the Jewish Interpreters*, Oxford, 1876 – 77. In *Light of the Lord*, Crescas used this verse in reference to the messiah; see III, 8, 1, p. 81a; 2, p. 82a – b; cf. also *Tanhuma*, Toledot, 14; *Yalkut Shimoni*, Isaiah, 476.

19. See Harvey, *Critique*, p. 142.

20. The syllogism is (1) if incarnation is impossible, then this redemption is impossible; (2) incarnation is impossible; therefore, (3) this redemption is impossible. That (2) is true will be proved in Chapter 4.

21. This principle is called "allopathy"; see Hyam Maccoby, *Judaism on Trial*, East Brunswick, N. J., 1982, pp. 220 – 221. The discussion there is based on Shlomo Ibn Verga, *Shevet Yehudah*, ed. by Y. Baer and A. Shochat, Jerusalem, 1947, p. 97. See also Thomas, *SCG*, IV, 53: "peccatum non expiatur peccato"; Regev, *Joseph*, p. 165.

22. Namely, by the crucifixion of Jesus.

23. Cf. Deut. 7:6; 14:2.

24. As per the third premise in Crescas' Preface.

25. Namely, the messiah, who is the choicest part of mankind, would be soiled by having to die to redeem humanity.

26. See n. 5.

27. Cf. Augustine, "Sermo XIII de Tempore," *PL*, 39:1997: "Factus est Deus homo ut homo fierit Deus."

CHAPTER 3
CONCERNING THE TRINITY

1. Christian theology distinguishes between the generation *(generatio)* of the Son and the procession *(processio)* of the Spirit; see Thomas, *Summa*, I, 27.

2. For the identification of the Christian persons of the trinity with divine attributes, see Harry A. Wolfson, *The Philosophy of the Kalam*, Cambridge, Mass., and London, 1976, pp. 112 – 132; *idem*, "Extradeical and Intradeical Interpretations of Platonic Ideas," *Religious Philosophy*, New York, 1965, pp. 27 – 68; Lasker, *Polemics,* pp. 51 – 76. This explanation of the trinity was not very widespread in normative Christian theological discussions, but it was used extensively in anti-Jewish polemics; see Lasker, *Polemics*, pp. 63 – 64 (including other examples of power, wisdom, and will).

3. The Christians recognized these "doubts and refutations"; see, e.g., Thomas, *SCG*, IV, 10 (the arguments) and 14 (his answers to them).

4. Hebrew *meḥuyyav ha-meẓi'ut*, literally, "the necessary of existence." This name for God has its origin in the philosophy of Abu Ali al-Hussein Ibn Sina (Avicenna, 980 – 1037), and it was widespread in Jewish philosophy; see Maimonides, *Guide*, I, 57; II, 1. Christians also used this term; see Thomas, *Summa*, I, 2, 3; *SCG*, I, 42.

5. See Thomas, *Summa*, I, 27, 2. Something which is dependent on something else for its existence cannot have necessary existence, since if the "something else" does not exist, the "something" cannot exist either.

6. For similar arguments, see Thomas, *SCG*, IV, 16; his answers to these objections are in IV, 23.

7. See Thomas, *Summa*, I, 4; *SCG*, I, 28.

8. Hebrew *be'attah*, literally "in an instant of time."

9. If generation were in time and not in an instant of time, then there must have been some time before generation; in that time before generation ("the first half of the time"), the Son was nonexistent. Therefore, the Son is not eternal.

10. Namely, the Son was generated in an instant of time.

11. Hebrew *ne'eẓal*, proceeded, emanated; Joseph ben Shem Tov should have written *nolad*.

12. *Physics* IV, 10 – 14; VI, 2, 232b, 20 – 233a, 32. In *Light of the Lord*, Crescas objected to Aristotle's definition of time, but he agreed that time was a continuous magnitude; see Harry A. Wolfson, *Crescas' Critique of Aristotle*, Cambridge, Mass., 1929, pp. 93 – 98, 282 – 291, 633 – 664; Warren Harvey, "The Term *Hitdabbekut* in Crescas' Definition of Time," *Jewish Quarterly Review*, 71:1 (1980 – 81): 44 – 47. See also Chapter 6. Thomas accepted Aristotle's definition of time; see Thomas, *Summa*, I, 53, 3; cf. also I, 10, 4 – 5; III, 75, 7. Maimonides wrote that the idea that time is composed of instants is one of the propositions of Kalamic physics; see *Guide*, I, 73, 3.

13. Hence, generation was neither in time nor in an instant, but from eternity, with the Father and Son both eternal; see Thomas, *Summa*, I, 42, 2. According to Crescas, this belief leads to the improper conclusion that time is composed of instants, as well as other impossible results: (1) the Son is destroyed in every instant; (2) the Son is generated and destroyed in every instant, and, therefore, exists and does not exist simultaneously; (3) the Son presently existent is not the one who existed even an instant ago.

In the following section Crescas generally uses pronouns to refer to the Father and the Son. The correct antecedents of the pronouns have been placed in brackets.

14. Hebrew *mi-she'ar ma'amarav*, literally, his other treatises (some manuscripts read "my other treatises"). Cf. Joseph ben Shem Tov's statement in his work *Kevod Elohim*, p. 7a: "That which I translated in these chapters from the tenth book of Aristotle's *Ethics* was translated according to my understanding of them. I did not see fit to translate his words literally, because [the book] is very profound and succinct. Yet I tried with all my might not to diverge from the essences of his words, [relying] instead on a slight expansion, so that it might be understood by many of our intellectuals, for very few of our nation can understand Aristotle's actual words without a commentary." On Crescas' style and Joseph's method of translation, see the Foreword to the English Translation.

15. There is no certainty that Crescas actually knew the writings of Abu Hamid Al-Ghazali (1058 – 1111), the well-known Muslim thinker, whose fierce criticism of philosophy was entitled *The Incoherence of the Philosophers (Tahafut al-Falasifah)*; see Wolfson, *Crescas'*, pp. 11 – 18; Seymour Feldman, "The Theory of Eternal Creation in Hasdai Crescas and Some of His Predecessors," *Viator*, 11(1980): 304 – 305. The particular argument used here was clearly taken by Crescas from Gersonides (discussed later).

16. Maurice Bouyges, ed., *Algazel Tahafot Al-Falasifat*, Beirut, 1927, pp. 49 – 51; English trans. by Sabih A. Kamali, *Al-Ghazali's Tahafut Al-Falasifah*, Lahore, 1958, pp. 34 – 35. According to our editions of this work, the present argument is found at the end of the first part of the first question. Interestingly, Al-Ghazali mentioned Jesus directly after this passage (Bouyges, p. 53; Kamali,

p. 36), but in a different context entirely. Don Isaac Abravanel mentioned neither the first chapter nor the fourth chapter but the third chapter (Bouyges, pp. 103 – 109; Kamali, pp. 68 – 73); see Abravanel, *Sefer Shamayim Hadashim*, Roedelheim, 1828 (reprinted Jerusalem, 1966/67), p. 28a.

17. Gersonides (Levi ben Gershom, 1288 – 1344), *Wars of the Lord*, VI,1, 7, Riva di Trento, 1560 (reprinted, n.p., n.d.), pp. 51d – 52a. This argument is much more developed in *Wars of the Lord* than in *The Incoherence of the Philosophers*, leaving no doubt that Crescas took it from Gersonides. Concerning this proof, see Jacob J. Staub, *The Creation of the World According to Gersonides*, Chico, Calif., 1982, pp. 29 – 30; Seymour Feldman, "Gersonides' Proofs for the Creation of the Universe," *Proceedings of the American Academy for Jewish Research*, 35 (1967): 120 – 125; Charles Touati, *La pensée philosophique et théologique de Gersonide*, Paris, 1973, pp. 176 – 179.

18. Apparently the reference is to al-Ghazali, not to Gersonides.

19. Hebrew *ne'ezal*, the same term used for procession of the Spirit.

20. The question is not whether the world has an agent but whether that agent preexisted the world and, therefore, the world was created; or, whether the cause of the world and the world were coexistent and both eternal. Al-Ghazali argued that if the agent of the world had made it eternally, then impossible consequences would result (e.g., time would be composed of instants).

21. Cf. Thomas, *Summa*, I, 19, 2 – 3; 46, 2.

22. Hebrew *mushpaʿ*.

23. In Aristotle's usage, this Greek term means the realization or complete expression of some function, or the condition in which a potentiality has become an actuality.

24. *Physics* III, 1, 201a, 10 – 11. Crescas dealt with this definition in *Light of the Lord*, I, 1, 5, p. 8b; see Wolfson, *Crescas'*, pp. 232 – 235, 521 – 530.

25. Hebrew *aẓilut.*

26. Only in respect to motion or light, which quickly pass out of existence, can one say that their agent makes them from beginning to end such that they are subject to continuous emanation. Existent bodies, e.g., the heavenly bodies, are not continuously activated by their agent. Instead, they were created at one discrete instant.

27. See Al-Ghazali, *Incoherence*, Bouyges, pp. 41 – 45; Kamali, pp. 27 – 30.

28. Since Crescas himself did not accept this proof (discussed later), it is possible that this is a personal attack by Joseph ben Shem Tov on Crescas. For Joseph's relation to Crescas, see Regev, *Joseph*, pp. 63 – 64; 120, n. 88.

29. III, 1, 4, pp. 67a – b (the proof is found in III, 1, 3, p. 63b); see Feldman, "Theory," pp. 304 – 319.

30. Even though Crescas wrote his book *Light of the Lord* in stages, and, therefore, some of the parts could have been written before *The Refutation*, Joseph ben Shem Tov's conclusion is not reasonable. Crescas' physical and metaphysical opinions are probably the product of his mature thought; see Rosenberg, "*Arba'ah Turim.*" *The Refutation* was written in 1398 (see the Foreword to the English Translation) and *Light of the Lord* was completed in 1410; see Wolfson, *Crescas'*, pp. 16 – 18. Isaac Abravanel accepted Joseph ben Shem Tov's opinion in this matter, but stated that Crescas' change of mind came about as a result of his having read Averroes' *Incoherence of the Incoherence*; see *Shamayim Ḥadashim*, p. 28a.

31. See Crescas' Preface: "so that the truth may be seen in the clearest manner, by eliminating all deception or equivocation." Nevertheless, there may be a difference between Crescas' stand concerning eternal creation in his polemical work and that in his philosophical work; see the Foreword to the English Translation.

32. I.e., until he composed the present work.

33. This composition apparently did not survive; see the list of Joseph ben Shem Tov's writings in Regev, *Joseph*, pp. 29 – 40.

34. Joseph ben Shem Tov used the same expression in *Kevod Elohim*, p. 19b.

The following section has no relation to the Jewish-Christian debate or to Hasdai Crescas' opinions. Joseph's purpose here is to show that Averroes (see n. 35) contradicted himself when he denied the creation of the world. To that end, Joseph cited a number of passages from the writings of Aristotle and Averroes.

35. The Muslim Abu Walid Ibn Rushd (Averroes, 1126 – 1198) was an outstanding Aristotelian, known especially for his commentaries on Aristotle's writings. His answer to Al-Ghazali's criticism of philosophy was *The Incoherence of the Incoherence (Tahafut at-Tahafut)*.

36. Maurice Bouyges, ed., *Tahafot At-Tahafot*, Beirut, 1930, p. 172; translated by Simon van den Bergh, *Averroes' Tahafut Al-Tahafut (The Incoherence of the Incoherence)*, London, 1954, p. 103.

37. *Ibid.*

38. Vatican Heb. ms. 283/12, f. 344; see also Maurice Bouyges, ed., *Averroes Tafsir Ma Ba'd At-Tabi'at*, vol. 3, Beirut, 1948, p. 1649; translated by Charles Genequand, *Ibn Rushd's Metaphysics*, Leiden, 1986, p. 172.

39. I.e., he raised a theoretical possibility which he knew not to be true, namely that the world could continue to exist without the existence of God.

40. Averroes, *Tahafut Al-Tahafut*, ed. Bouyges, pp. 165 – 169; van den Bergh, pp. 99 – 101. See also Harry A. Wolfson, "The Plurality of Immovable Movers in Aristotle, Averroes, and St. Thomas," *Harvard Studies in Classical Philology*, 63 (1958): 243 – 249 (reprinted in *Studies*, I, pp. 11 – 17). The argument here is that although the world could conceivably exist without a God Who maintained it, the intellects must have God for their existence, since they exist by virtue of their cognizing their cause, i.e., God.

41. In *On the Heavens*, II, Aristotle dealt with the motions and forms of the heavens, the stars, and the earth, but his purpose was to show that the world is eternal. It is possible that Joseph ben Shem Tov was influenced here by the statement of Gersonides,

Wars of the Lord, VI, 1, 8 – 9, that the heavenly bodies exist for a purpose and were, therefore, created.

42. Joseph ben Shem Tov apparently took this expression from *Wars of the Lord*, VI, 1, 9, p. 53a. Crescas used the same expression in *Light of the Lord*, p. 55b.

43. According to Joseph, if Averroes admitted that the world has an agent, he would also have to admit that the world was created. Averroes refused to admit that the world was created because he thought that Aristotle's arguments for the eternity of the world were convincing. For Averroes' theory of eternal creation, see Barry S. Kogan, *Averroes and the Metaphysics of Causation*, Albany, 1985, pp. 203 – 265.

44. The order of the premises here is different from their order in Crescas' Preface.

45. Hebrew *ma'alot*. For the divine attributes, see Thomas, *Summa*, I, 4 (*perfectus*); 10 (*aeternitas*); 14 (*scientia*); 18 (*vita*); 19 (*voluntas*); and 25 (*potentia*).

46. A similar argument is used by Saadia Gaon, *Beliefs and Opinions*, II, 5 (in uncensored editions); and in Nahmanides' account of the Disputation of Barcelona in C. D. Chavel, ed., *Kitvei Rabbeinu Moshe ben Naḥman*, vol. I, Jerusalem, 1962/63, p. 320.

47. See Augustine, *De Trinitate*, VI, 4 – 8, *PL*, 42:927 – 930; Fourth Lateran Council, in Henrici Denziger, *Enchiridion Symbolorum (Denz.)*, various editions, no. 428; Thomas, *Summa*, I, 3 (esp. 7). See also *Light of the Lord*, I, 3, 4, p. 26a.

48. See *Light of the Lord*, I, 1, 1, p. 7b; Wolfson, *Crescas'*, pp. 63 – 64, 191, 423 – 424; *idem, The Philosophy of Spinoza*, Cambridge, Mass., 1961, pp. 286 – 295; Rosenberg, "*Arba'ah Turim*," p. 534.

Christians agreed with this premise; see Thomas, *Summa*, III, 10, 3; Nicolas Cusanus (Nicholas of Cusa), *Of Learned Ignorance*, trans. by Germain Heron, London, 1954, p. 36.

49. Thomas, *Summa*, I, 3, 7.

50. I.e., immediately above.

51. I.e., cause the Spirit to proceed.

52. Cf. the Fourth Lateran Council, *Denz.*, 432; Thomas, *SCG*, IV, 14.

53. For similar arguments, see Lasker, *Polemics*, pp. 71 – 72.

54. Cf. the following section with Joseph ben Shem Tov, *Commentary on the Epistle*, p. 50; Lasker, *Polemics*, pp. 92, 219 – 220.

55. *Metaphysics*, VII, 6, 1031a, 15 – 1032a, 11. (The numbering of the books of Aristotle's *Metaphysics* was different in the Middle Ages.)

56. As contrasted with the intelligible essence, namely, manhood, which exists only in the intellect.

57. There is a distinction between the general essence of something, e.g., humanity, and its individual essence, e.g., the individual Reubenness of this particular Reuben. Reuben's individual essence is "Reuben," but he also participates with all other humans in the general essence of humanity. A Father, Son, and Spirit which have the same general essence, but each one of whom has its own independent individual essence, are three gods; if they have only one individual essence, then one cannot distinguish between the Persons because they are all one thing.

58. Hebrew *ḥilluf*, another possible translation is "alternation." This term translates the Latin *diversitas* or *differentia*, and Christians agreed that such terms cannot be attributed to God; see Thomas, *Summa*, I, 31, 2, in which he said that God has no *diversitas* or *differentia*, but He does have *distinctio*. For this argument, see Lasker, *Polemics*, p. 209, n. 208; see also Rosenberg, "*Arba'ah Turim*," p. 566.

59. See Thomas, *SCG*, IV, 10, 14. Crescas' conclusion about infinite, internal inconsistency does not seem to follow necessarily from his arguments.

60. See Augustine, *De Fide et Symbolo*, I:9, *PL*, 40:193; the Council of Rheims, *Denz.*, no. 391; Peter Lombard, *Sententiae*, I, 8, 9, *PL* 192:545 – 546; Thomas, *Summa*, I, 3, 3; 27, 3; John of Salisbury, *Historia Pontificalis*, 8.

61. For a similar argument, see Anselm, *Monologium* 60 – 62, in *Opera Omnia*, vol. 1, pp. 70 – 73; Lombard, *Sententiae*, I, 10, *PL* 192:549 – 551 (and Thomas' *Commentary, ad loc.*); Thomas, *Summa*, I, 30, 2; *idem, De Potentia*, 9, 9.

62. A discussion of the following passage is in Lasker, *Polemics*, pp. 69 – 74.

63. Maimonides, *Guide*, I, 50 – 60.

64. See Al-Ghazali, *Tahafut*, ed. Bouyges, p. 150; Kamali, p. 100.

65. See Averroes, *Tahafut Al-Tahafut*, Bouyges, pp. 297 – 302; van den Bergh, pp. 176 – 179.

66. *Light of the Lord*, I, 3, 3, pp. 22b – 26a; Wolfson, "Problem," *JQR*, pp. 198 – 221 (*Studies*, vol. II, pp. 314 – 337). Crescas specifically polemicized against the Christian trinity in *Light of the Lord*, p. 25a – b.

It is possible that the Christian doctrine of the trinity influenced Crescas' theory of attributes; see Shlomo Pines, "Scholasticism after Thomas Aquinas and the Teachings of Hasdai Crescas and His Predecessors," in *Proceedings of the Israel Academy of Sciences and Humanities*, 1, 10 (1967).

67. I.e., a trinitarian.

68. Abraham Shalom (d. 1492) strongly criticized Crescas' theory of attributes, but we do not know whether he wrote his *Neveh Shalom* before Joseph ben Shem Tov's translation of *The Refutation* in 1451. In addition, Shalom did not deal in his criticism with Christian aspects. It is difficult to know to whom Joseph ben Shem Tov referred here. See *Sefer Neveh Shalom*, Venice, 1574/75 (reprinted, Jerusalem, 1966/67), pp. 200b – 208a.

69. This philological point is correct, since the word *parẓof* comes from the Greek *prosopon*, meaning mask, which was translated into the Latin *persona*. Greek-speaking Christians used the term *prosopon* for the Father, the Son, and the Spirit; Latin-speaking Christians translated it as *persona*.

70. Hebrew *be-'aẓmuto zeh*, literally, "in this, his essence."

71. See, e.g., *Light of the Lord*, I, 3, 3; Al-Ghazali, *Tahafut*, ed. Bouyges, p. 150; Kamali, p. 100; Nahmanides, "Disputation of Barcelona," p. 320; Kalman Bland, ed., *The Epistle on the Possibility of Conjunction with the Active Intellect by Ibn Rushd with the Commentary of Moses Narboni*, New York, 1982, p. 72 (Heb.), 64 (Eng.); Duran, *Disgrace*, p. 15; Lasker, *Polemics*, p. 64.

72. Maimonides, *Guide*, I, 50 – 60, argued that the belief in positive attributes is tantamount to a belief in God's corporeality.

73. See n. 66.

74. Crescas is, thus, not a trinitarian despite his theory of positive attributes which posited that God has power, wisdom, and will.

CHAPTER 4
CONCERNING INCARNATION

1. The classical Christian description of the need for incarnation is found in Anselm, *Cur Deus Homo*, pp. 37-133. For Jewish philosophical arguments against incarnation, see Lasker, *Polemics*, pp. 105 – 134, 225 – 240.

2. Hebrew *beten*, literally, belly, used for both stomach and womb.

3. Thomas, *Summa*, III, 50, 2.

4. This imagery is quite old in Christianity; see the *Quicumque Vult Credo*, in *Denz.*, no. 40; Thomas, *Summa*, III, 2, 9. See also Duran, *Disgrace*, p. 9

5. I.e., the reason for incarnation.

6. I.e., the form of the incarnation.

7. See Thomas, *SCG*, IV, 53; *Summa*, III, 1, 2. See also Chapter 2 in which Crescas used the same argument as here.

8. Thomas, *Summa*, III, 2, 1; *SCG*, IV, 35, more or less agreed with the following analysis, yet he still accepted the doctrine of incarnation. Christians were able to find a model for divine-human conjunction by positing the existence of a special type of conjunction called "hypostatic union."

9. See Thomas, *Summa*, III, 1, 1.

10. See Crescas' Preface.

11. Cf. Aristotle, *Metaphysics*, XII, 4, 1070b, 5 – 6. Thomas agreed that something which is composed is different from its constituent elements; see *SCG* , IV, 35.

12. Aristotle, *On Generation and Corruption*, I, 10, 327b, 34 – 328a, 9.

13. *Idem*, *Metaphysics*, VIII, 2, 1042b, 16.

14. *Ibid.*, 19.

15. Such as the soul and the body; see *ibid.*, *On the Soul*, II, 1, 412a, 16 – 21. Crescas' discussion of the types of unity is not particularly comprehensive; see also Aristotle, *On Generation and Corruption*, I, 10, 327a, 29 – 328b, 25; Harry A. Wolfson, *The Philosophy of the Church Fathers*, vol. 1, Cambridge, Mass., 1964, pp. 372 – 386.

16. Apparently, the second proof that "this person ... would be another substance, composed of these two natures" is missing.

17. See Joseph ben Shem Tov, *Commentary on the Epistle*, pp. 60 – 64.

18. If He is God, He cannot be a corporeal form; if He is a corporeal form, He cannot be God.

19. For Thomas' answers, see *Summa*, III, 1, 1, ad 1; 2, 1.

20. Literally, "belly" (and in the following).

21. See also Duran, *Disgrace*, p. 10.

22. See Regev, *Joseph*, pp. 78, 80, 107.

23. Literally, "Also it would not be said about this conjunction — it is it (*hu' hu'*)"; see Harvey, *Critique*, pp. 302, 478, n. 1.

24. Regev, *Joseph,* pp. 74, 80, 98, 107, 117.

25. Aristotle, *Physics*, VIII, 10, 267b, 8.

26. See *Aristotelis Opera cum Averrois Commentarius*, vol. 4, Venice 1562 (reprinted, Frankfurt am Main, 1962), pp. 432a – b.

God cannot be in a place, since He is incorporeal. When one says, nevertheless, that He is in the outermost sphere, it means that He is conjoined with that sphere with "conjunction of existence," namely God gives existence to the motion of the sphere.

27. Any connection, love, or providence between God and man would not cause true conjunction because God is not corporeal. Crescas analyzed the various meanings of union; Joseph, here, completed the discussion by analyzing the various meanings of conjunction.

28. Such as body and soul; see Regev, *Joseph*, p. 107.

29. Averroes' opinion can be found in Averroes, *Averrois Cordubensis Commentarium Magnum in Aristotelis de Anima Libros*, ed. by F. Stuart Crawford, Cambridge, Mass., 1953, pp. 436 – 454. It is unclear whether Joseph ben Shem Tov saw Averroes' Long Commentary on *On the Soul*; see Harry A. Wolfson, "Plan for the Publication of a *Corpus Commentariorum Averrois in Aristotelem*," in *Studies*, vol. I, pp. 430 – 454. Therefore, the reference is probably to the Middle Commentary; see Paris Ms. 947 (Institute of Microfilmed Hebrew Manuscripts, film no. 32600), ff. 218b – 224a. For Averroes' psychology, see also J. Hercz, ed., *Drei Abhandlungen über die Conjunction des separaten Intellects mit dem menschen*, Berlin, 1869; Herbert Davidson, "Averroes on the Material Intellect," *Viator*, 17 (1986): 91 – 137.

30. Abner of Burgos actually did argue something similar in his *Sefer Teshuvot La-Meharef*, Parma ms. 2440, ff. 21a – 25b. See also Baer, *History*, vol. 1, pp. 344 – 45; Lasker, *Polemics*, p. 129; Shoshana G. Gershenzon, *A Study of* Teshuvot La-Meharef *of Abner of Burgos*, D.H.L. dissertation, Jewish Theological Seminary, 1984.

31. Joseph ben Shem Tov meant that if it is possible to answer the question, What is he? in reference to Jesus with the answer, God, then God is part of the definition of Jesus. Jesus was composed of form and matter. It is clear that the matter was not God; it follows, therefore, that according to the Christians, the form of Jesus was God, and his matter was man.

32. *Wars of the Lord*, I, 4, pp. 6a – 7b; Levi Ben Gershom (Gersonides), *The Wars of the Lord*, trans. by Seymour Feldman, vol. 1, Philadelphia, 1984, p. 130 – 143. Generally, Joseph ben Shem Tov was critical of Gersonides but appreciative of Averroes; see Regev, *Joseph*, pp. 57 – 60, 62 – 63, 170, n. 40.

33. Jer. 5:12.

34. Ex. 15:11.

35. *Aleph, lamed, mem* instead of *aleph, lamed, yod, mem;* the defective form can also mean dumb (speechless).

36. Cf. B. Gittin, p. 56b.

37. For this expression, based on Job 23:3, see Wolfson, *Crescas'*, p. 417, n. 30.

38. According to the Christians, the body of Jesus is physically present in the heavens; see Thomas, *Summa*, III, 58.

39. See *ibid.*, 3, 4.

40. Cf. Joseph ben Shem Tov, *Commentary on the Epistle*, pp. 56 – 60. See also Duran, *Epistle*, p. 75. For the issue of divine unity, change, and incarnation, see Lasker, *Polemics*, pp. 114 – 125, 230 – 236.

41. Hebrew *ḥokhmat ha-devarim;* literally, "the science of words" (and see n. 42). See also, Wolfson, *Kalam*, pp. 43 – 64; Shlomo Pines, "Some Traits of Christian Theological Writing in Relation to Moslem *Kalam* and to Jewish Thought," *Proceedings of the Israel Academy of Sciences and Humanities*, 5, Jerusalem, 1976, pp. 105 – 118.

42. Theology ("speech about God") is equivalent to Islamic Kalam (literally, "speech" or "word"). On the relation between Kalam and theology, see Wolfson, "The Twice-Revealed Averroes," in James F. Ross, ed., *Inquiries into Medieval Philosophy: A Collection in Honor of Francis P. Clarke*, Westport, Conn., 1971, p. 221 (reprinted in *Studies*, II, p. 381).

43. *Guide*, I, 50.

44. Paris ms. 956, ff. 485a – 486a.

45. Bland edition, pp. 29 – 30, 34 – 36, 43 – 44, 47 (Hebrew); 37 – 38, 40 – 41, 45 – 46, 48 (English). Joseph ben Shem Tov wrote two commentaries on *The Epistle on the Possibility of Conjunction*, one long (still unpublished) and one short; see Shaul Regev, "Joseph ibn Shem Tov's Short Commentary of Averroes' 'Epistle on the Possibility of Conjunction,'" *Jerusalem Studies in Jewish Thought*, I:2 (1982): 38 – 93 (in Hebrew). For Joseph's relation to Averroes' psychology, see Regev, *Joseph*, pp. 74 – 138.

46. Cf. I Kings 22:22, 23; II Chron. 18:21, 22.

47. Thomas, *Summa*, III, 50, 2.

48. Literally, "hanged." See also, Duran, *Disgrace*, p. 10.

49. *Metaphysics*, XII, 7, 1072b, 25 – 29.

50. See Thomas, *Summa*, III, 50, 2, ad 3.

51. Perhaps the reference here is to *Posterior Analytics*, I, 4; *Metaphysics*, VII, 6.

52. Conceptualization is possible by apprehending the abstract essences. There are things whose abstract essences exist only in the intellect (e.g., the essence of a table or a chair), and there are things which are incorporeal (e.g., intellects) whose abstract essences exist outside the intellect. The question of the status of the essences is one of the issues which divide Platonism from Aristotelianism.

53. *On the Soul*, III, 4 – 8.

54. *Metaphysics*, XII, 7, 1072b, 14 – 1073a, 12; 9, 1074b, 15 – 1075a, 11 (on Joseph's chapter number, see Chapter 3, n. 55).

55. If God's powers of life and comprehension are a result of His incorporeality, it follows, therefore, that these powers could not exist in someone who is not incorporeal.

56. Thomas, *SCG*, IV, 53, 55.

57. It is unclear why this argument is the second one because it is not preceded by an argument labeled "the first argument." The rest of the arguments in this chapter are found in Thomas, *Summa*, III, 50, 2, 3, and 5.

58. See n. 37.

59. Is. 31:3.

60. Cf. John 2:4. Generally, the Jewish polemicists argued that Jesus observed the commandments, in order to argue that according to the New Testament, the Torah is not abrogated; see, e.g., Duran, *Disgrace*, pp. 24 – 34.

CHAPTER 5
CONCERNING VIRGIN BIRTH

1. The Latin terms are *ante partum, in partu*, and *post partum*. This formulation of the Christian belief can be found, e.g., in Augustine, *Sermo CXCV, PL* 39:2107; see also the statement of the First Lateran Council, *Denz.*, 256; Thomas, *Summa*, III, 28. For the history of this Christian doctrine, see Hilda Graef, *Mary: A History of Doctrine and Devotion*, 2 vols., New York, 1963 – 65; Paul F. Palmer, *Mary in the Documents of the Church*, Westminster, Md., 1952. Crescas' arguments here refer only to the belief that Mary remained a virgin at the time of the birth (*in partu*). For a review of Jewish philosophical arguments against virgin birth, see Lasker, *Polemics*, pp. 153 – 159, 251 – 255.

2. See Wolfson, *Crescas'*, pp. 261, 590 – 591.

3. I, 1.

4. In other words, every body has three dimensions, and anything which has three dimensions is a body; see Aristotle, *Posterior Analytics*, II, 4, 91a, 16. See also *Light of the Lord*, I, 1, 5, p. 8b; Wolfson, *Crescas'*, pp. 233, 526.

5. Hebrew *reḥem*, (and in the following).

6. A similar argument can be found in Thomas, *Summa*, III, 28, 2.

7. Such an idea is mentioned as well in Joseph ben Shem Tov's *Commentary on the Epistle*, pp. 98 – 100. Thomas, *Summa*, III, 28, 2, ad 3, rejected this concept, but it was accepted by Innocent III, *De Sacro Altaris Mysterio*, IV, 12, *PL*, 217:864.

8. The source of this argument is Aristotle, *Physics*, IV, 1, 208b, 6 – 8; 8, 216a, 26 – 216b, 12; *On Generation and Corruption*, I, 5, 321a, 8 – 10. Though Crescas did not accept completely the Aristotelian view of matter, he did agree that the interpenetrability of bodies is impossible; see *Light of the Lord*, I, 1, 1; 2, 1; Wolfson, *Crescas'*, pp. 146 – 149, 184 – 187, 342 – 343, 415 – 418.

9. Aristotle, *Physics*, IV, 12, 221a, 22 – 23, used the term "grain of millet." The expression "grain of mustard seed" might be taken from Matt. 17:20 or Luke 17:6 (and see Duran, *Disgrace*, p. 55; Maimonides, *Guide*, I:56). See also Wolfson, *Crescas'*, pp. 146 – 147, 342 – 343. This expression is found as well in Duran, *Epistle*, p. 76.

10. I.e., not through the birth canal. There were Christians who believed that Jesus was, indeed, born at another place in Mary's body; see Ratramnus, *De Eo Quod Christus ex Virgine Natus Est, PL*, 121:81 – 102; Frank Talmage, "An Hebrew Polemical Treatise, Anti-Cathar and Anti-Orthodox," *Harvard Theological Review*, 60 (1967): 341 (but cf. David Berger, "Christian Heresy and Jewish Polemic in the Twelfth and Thirteenth Centuries," *Harvard Theological Review*, 69 [1975]: 287 – 303).

CHAPTER 6
CONCERNING TRANSUBSTANTIATION

1. Hebrew *zeviḥat mizbaḥam*, literally, "the sacrifice of their altar."

2. For a description of the Christian belief, see Crescas' Preface, and Duran, *Disgrace*, pp. 35 – 36. The Jewish philosophical arguments against transubstantiation are discussed in Lasker, *Polemics*, pp. 135 – 151, 240 – 251.

3. In Chapter 3.

4. In Chapter 4.

5. Hebrew *'ugah*, see Crescas' Preface, n. 21.

6. If God were created and destroyed, He would not have necessary existence (see Chapter 3).

7. A similar argument is found in Thomas, *SCG*, IV, 63; Duran, *Epistle*, p. 77.

8. Thomas, *Summa*, III, 75, 7.

9. See Duran, *Disgrace*, p. 36; this calculation is apparently based on J. Berakhot 9:1 (13a); see also, *Guide*, III, 14.

10. Cf. Ps. 33:14.

11. *Physics*, IV, 11; VI, 3 – 4. See also *ibid.*, IV, 8, 216a, 12 – 216b, 12; *On the Heavens*, I, 6, 273a, 21 – 274a, 18; Wolfson, *Crescas'*, pp. 144 – 147, 341 – 342.

12. *Physics*, VI, 4, 235a, 34 – 235b, 6. Joseph ben Shem Tov adduced the same sources in *Commentary on the Epistle*, p. 90.

13. Aristotle's definition of time is in *Physics*, IV, 11, 219b, 1 – 2. In *Light of the Lord*, I, 2, 7, Crescas criticized this definition; see Wolfson, *Crescas'*, pp. 93 – 98, 285 – 291, 636 – 640, 646 – 664. Cf., also, Harvey, "Term." In any event, Crescas agreed that instantaneous motion is impossible.

14. See Crescas' Preface and *Light of the Lord*, II, 3.

15. See Duran, *Epistle*, pp. 77 – 78.

16. *On the Heavens*, I, 2 – 3.

17. Hebrew *ḥalulim, neqavim*. This expression is borrowed from the *Asher yaẓar* blessing from the morning service, also said after bodily elimination. Since Crescas wrote in the vernacular, it is impossible to know whether this expression, which occurs in the same context in Duran, *Epistle*, p. 77, is Crescas' or Joseph ben Shem Tov's. See also Lasker, *Polemics*, p. 142.

18. This explanation of transubstantiation is offered by Bonaventura, *Commentary on Sententiae*, IV, Dist. 11, 1; Albertus Magnus, *De Sacramentis*, V, 1, q. 1, a. 2, and q. 4, a. 1, in *Opera Omnia*, 26, Aschendorff, 1958, pp. 51, 62; William of Auvergne, *Tractatus Guilhermi Parisiensis de Sacramentis Cur Deus Homo*, 1496, fol. 26a; see also Salvatore Bonano, *The Concept of Substance and the Development of Eucharistic Theology to the Thirteenth Century*, Washington, D.C., 1960, pp. 25, 39; Lasker, *Polemics*, pp. 142 – 143,

246 – 247; *idem*, "Transubstantiation, Elijah's Chair, Plato, and the Jewish-Christian Debate," *Revue des Études Juives*, 143:1 – 2 (January – June, 1984): 31 – 58.

Crescas mentioned the concept of the "glorified body" also in the context of virgin birth; see Chapter 5. This connection was made by Hugh of St. Victor, *Summa Sententiarum*, VI, 4, *PL*, 176:141; see, in addition, A. J. Macdonald, "Berengar and the Virgin Birth," *Journal of Theological Studies*, 30 (1929): 293; Joseph ben Shem Tov, *Commentary on the Epistle*, pp. 98 – 100.

19. Thomas, *Summa*, III, 75, 1; *SCG*, IV, 62; Lasker, *Polemics*, pp. 144 – 145; *idem*, "Transubstantiation."

20. Though the order here appears to be incorrect, all of the manuscripts list "hundreds" last, and this is the order in Duran, *Epistle*, p. 77, where there is a very similar argument.

21. Christians did not agree with this argument; see Thomas, *Summa*, III, 75, 5; 77, 1; *SCG*, IV, 62; Lombard, *Sententiae*, Dist. 12, 1, *PL*, 192:864; William Ockham, *De Corpore Christi*, in *The De Sacramento Altaris of William of Occam*, ed. by T. Bruce Birch, Burlington, Iowa, 1930, pp. 240 – 245; 284 – 285; G. Buescher, *The Eucharistic Teaching of William Ockham*, St. Bonaventure, New York, 1950, pp. 119 – 140. See also Duran, *Epistle*, p. 78.

22. If the properties of the bread are only accidents, they should not be nutrients; see Aristotle, *On the Soul*, II, 4, 416b, 12; Thomas, *Summa*, III, 75, 4, and 6; Duran, *Epistle*, p. 78; Lasker, *Polemics*, p. 149.

23. See Duran, *Epistle*, pp. 76 – 79; *Disgrace*, p. 36.

24. For Joseph's commentary on Duran's arguments against transubstantiation, see *Commentary on the Epistle*, pp. 84 – 128.

25. Jer. 16:20.

26. Cf. Matt. 26:26 – 28; Mark 14:22 – 24; Luke 22:19 – 20.

27. Thomas, *Summa*, III, 76, 6; see also Alger of Liège, *De Sacramentis Corporis et Sanguinis Dominici*, 14, *PL*, 180:780; A. J. Macdonald, *Berengar and the Reform of the Sacramental Doctrine*, London, 1930, p. 393.

28. Job 12:6.

29. Reference here is to the Feast of Corpus Christi; see the description of Shlomo ibn Verga, *Shevet Yehudah*, p. 123; Herbert Thurston, "Exposition of the Blessed Sacrament," *Catholic Encyclopedia*, 5, New York, 1909, pp. 713 – 714. Crescas was himself accused once of host desecration; see Baer, *History*, II, 38 – 41.

CHAPTER 7
CONCERNING BAPTISM

1. Hebrew *ha-ʿiqqar . . . laʿaqor*, a play on words.

2. The baptized child needs a patron; see Thomas, *Summa*, III, 67, 7 – 8.

3. Hebrew *lo ʿaltah tevilah be-yado*. This expression is borrowed from the Talmud, B. Hullin 10a, Niddah 67a.

4. Hebrew *tevul yom*, this expression was used by Duran to describe (apparently derogatively) New Christians. It is borrowed from M. Tevul Yom, which deals with someone who has immersed himself to become ritually pure but is not yet purified because night has not fallen; see Duran, *Epistle*, p. 81 (and n. 129).

5. Even babies need baptism; see Thomas, *Summa*, III, 68, 9. For another example of this Jewish argument, see David Berger, *The Jewish-Christian Debate in the High Middle Ages*, Philadelphia, 1979, Eng. section, p. 312.

6. Job 34:10.

7. Cf. Ez. 18:20: "The son shall not suffer for the iniquity of the father." See also Thomas, *SCG*, IV, 51; *Summa*, I – II, 81, 1.

8. See Thomas, *Summa*, III, 68, 3. In a new edition of this work, there is an echo of the arguments which are used here by Crescas; see *Summa Theologiae*, vol. 57: *Baptism and Confirmation*, trans. and ed. by James J. Cunningham, New York – London, 1976, pp. 88 – 89, note A; appendix 3, pp. 235 – 238.

CHAPTER 8
CONCERNING THE COMING OF THE MESSIAH

1. This follows the Christian view. According to Jewish sources, the Urim and Tumim did not exist during the Second Temple, and prophecy ended with Malachi, at least a few hundred years before Jesus. See Ephraim E. Urbach, *"Matai Pasqah Ha-Nevu'ah,"* *Tarbiz*, 17 (1945/46): 1 – 11; B. Sotah, 48a – b; B. Yoma 21b; *Seder Olam Zuta*, ed. by Menachem Grossberg, London, 1909/10 (reprinted, Jerusalem, 1969/70), p. 26. Crescas argued that the belief that "the High Priest is answered by the Urim and Tumim" is one of the true beliefs of Judaism; see *Light of the Lord*, III, 7.

2. Prophecy is an end in itself and is not necessary in order to instill belief in the people; for Crescas' theory of prophecy, see *Light of the Lord*, II, 4.

3. In *Light of the Lord*, II, 2, 1, Crescas argued that prophecy is part of divine providence.

4. The Great Schism in Western Christianity lasted from September 20, 1378, to November 8, 1417. See E. Vansteenberghe, "Schisme d'occident (grande)," *Dictionnaire de théologie catholique*, vol. 14, pt. 1, Paris, 1939, cols. 1468 – 1492. See also Duran, *Epistle*, p. 81: "I do not know if he will go to Rome or he will find rest in Avignon."

5. Matt. 10:16; 15:21 – 28; Mark 7:24 – 30.

6. Thomas also asked why incarnation was not clear for all; see *SCG*, IV, 53. See also Berger, *Debate*, pp. 43 – 44, 236 – 237.

7. Luke 23:34.

CHAPTER 9
CONCERNING THE NEW TORAH

1. A number of the ideas of this chapter are developed in Crescas' *Light of the Lord*, II, 6.

2. The order here is different from that in Crescas' Preface. The other two premises are recorded later in the chapter.

3. See Thomas, *Summa*, I – II, 107, 2.

4. Crescas argued that the Christian belief is based on the following syllogism: (1) Everything perfected by something else is not in itself perfect; (2) The Torah of Moses was perfected by the New Testament; therefore, (3) The Torah of Moses is not perfect. According to Crescas, if the conclusion (3) is false, this proves that the preceding assumption (2) is also false.

5. The Christians claimed that the Torah of Moses was perfect for its purpose, namely, preparation for the coming of Jesus, but not absolutely perfect, since its purpose is not perfect in relation to the purpose of obtaining eternal life; see Thomas, *Summa*, I – II, 98, 2.

6. Namely, the Children of Israel, and not in relation to the Agent, namely God.

7. Hebrew *ʿavodat ha-miẓriyyim*, perhaps "Egyptian religion."

8. I.e., not the promise of the true good, namely, intellectual permanence after death.

9. Crescas mentioned a similar argument in *Light of the Lord*, III, 5, 1, p. 78b.

10. Hebrew "ve-neʿetaq ha-yeshivah ha-kolelet mei-ha-ḥokhmah asher hayetah be-khol ereẓ miẓrayim, ve-nish'ar kol oto ha-zeman asher hayu avoteihem sham."

11. B. Nedarim 32a; Genesis Rabba 39, 1. Crescas' statement here agrees with his opinion in *Light of the Lord*, I, 3, 6, p. 27b, that knowledge of God is achieved through prophecy and not through the intellect; see Harvey, "Crescas versus Maimonides." Concerning the heritage of Abraham, see also *Light of the Lord*, III, 3, 3, p. 74a.

12. Gen. 21:33 (in the context of Abraham's dealings with Avimelekh; cf. 12:8; 13:4). See also Maimonides, *Mishneh Torah*, "Laws of Idolatry," 1, 3.

13. Gen. 18:19.

14. Leviticus Rabba, 32, 5.

15. Deut. 7:6; 14:2. Crescas understood the situation in Egypt in light of his own experience in Spain, as if the Children of Israel could have escaped oppression by means of conversion. This way of understanding history was not unique to Crescas; see Peter Burke, *The Renaissance Sense of the Past*, London, 1969, pp. 1 – 6; Avraham Gross, "The Iberian Expulsions as Reflected in the Commentary on Esther," *Proceedings of the Ninth World Congress of Jewish Studies*, section II, vol. 1, Jerusalem, 1985/86, pp. 153 – 158. See also Rosenberg, "*Arba'ah Turim*," p. 549, and Crescas' statement in *Light of the Lord*, III, 3, 3, p. 74a.

16. Deut. 7:19; 29:2.

17. Hebrew *dat*, also, "religion"; see Joseph Albo, *Sefer Ha-'Ikkarim*, ed. Isaac Husik, vol. 1, Philadelphia, 1946, p. 2, n. 1. The belief that the Torah was intended to fit the needs of the generation which left Egypt is not solely a Christian belief but was held as well by Maimonides. The latter argued (*Guide*, III, 26 – 35) that many commandments were given to Israel not because of their intrinsic value but because of the low intellectual and spiritual level of that generation. This passage, then, must be seen as a polemic also against Maimonides' theory of the reasons for the commandments. For Crescas' own theory of the reasons for the commandments, see Isaac Heinemann, *Ta'amei Ha-Mizvot Be-Sifrut Yisrael*, vol. 1, Jerusalem, 1965/66, pp. 102 – 112. Cf. also the statement of Shem Tov Ibn Shaprut (Jewish polemicist, contemporary with Hasdai Crescas), *Sefer Even Bohan*, Medicea-Laurenziana Ms. Plut. 2,17 (Institute Film 17662), f. 11a: "Know that at the time of the giving of the Torah, most of the people of Israel were of gross intellects and thick brains, like workers of the land who had no other experience except for mortar and bricks."

18. *Light of the Lord*, p. 52a; see also *Guide*, I, 68.

19. Cf. Maimonides' theory of the reasons for the commandments, *Guide*, III, 26 – 34. Christian thinkers did not deny that there was value in the commandments but maintained that the purpose of the "Old Testament" was not equal to that of the New Testament; see Thomas, *Summa*, I – II, 101 – 102. One may assume that Christian missionaries, against whom Crescas wrote

this defense of the Torah of Moses, did not admit that the commandments had any value.

20. Cf. Ps. 121:4.

21. Ex. 7:22; 8:3, 14 – 15.

22. The survival of the Jewish people is often used as proof of the truth of the Jewish religion; see, e.g., Judah Halevi, *Kuzari*, II, 32 – 33.

23. Ex. 34:24.

24. B. Pesahim 8b; J. Peah 3:8; *Mekhilta of Rabbi Simeon bar Yohai*, ed. by Jacob Nahum Halevi Epstein and Ezra Zion Melammed, Jerusalem, 1954/55, p. 223.

25. Lev. 25:20 – 21.

26. Hebrew *'am ha-'arez;* literally, "the people of the land," used to designate ignoramuses.

27. Cf. Num. 5:27.

28. Cf. Num. 5:28.

29. See also Maimonides, *Guide*, III, 47; Nahmanides, *Commentary on the Torah*, ad Num. 5:13. Crescas mentioned these three miracles together a number of times in *Light of the Lord*; see II, 2, 3, p. 36b; III, 3, 1, p. 72a; also pilgrimage with Sotah, p. 57a and p. 82b; pilgrimage with sabbatical year, p. 81a. With these examples Crescas stressed that even those without intellectual accomplishments or knowledge of the Torah participated in the miracles.

The connection here between miracles and specific commandments may be seen as parallel to the connection made in *Light of the Lord*, III, part 2, between certain true beliefs and specific commandments.

30. M. Avot, 5:5.

31. Deut. 4:44.

32. The distinction between hidden and manifest miracles is made by Nahmanides; see David Berger, "Miracles and the Natu-

ral Order in Nahmanides," in Isadore Twersky, ed., *Rabbi Moses Nahmanides (Ramban): Explorations in His Religious and Literary Virtuosity*, Cambridge, Mass., and London, 1983, pp.107 – 128.

33. See Judah Halevi, *Kuzari*, I, 13; *Guide*, II, 36, 40; Joseph Albo, *Sefer Ha-ʿIkkarim*, I, 5 – 11.

34. See Maimonides, *Treatise on Logic*, 14.

35. Acts of the Apostles 7:14.

36. Gen. 46:27 (and cf. Ex. 1:5; Deut. 10:22); see also Duran, *Disgrace*, pp. 57 – 58; *Epistle*, p. 80.

37. The Jews must have heard the Christians refer to the authors of the Gospels as saints, and, as a result, this designation was used here.

38. Matt. 1:7 – 16 (descended from Solomon) and Luke (not John) 3:23 – 31 (descended from Nathan). This argument is found in quite a number of polemics; see Berger, *Debate*, Eng. section, p. 310; Duran, *Disgrace*, p. 54.

39. For other examples of arguments concerning contradictions in the New Testament, see Duran, *Disgrace*, pp. 49 – 59.

40. Is. 7:14; see Matt. 1:23. For similar arguments, see Berger, *Debate*, Heb. section, pp. 57 – 59.

41. Literally, "God is with us."

42. The chronology is according to *Seder Olam Zuta* (pp. 18, 32); see also Duran, *Disgrace*, p. 8; *Epistle*, p. 75. For Jewish views of the dates of Jesus, see *Disgrace*, pp. 60 – 63, and Talmage, *Polemical Writings*, pp. 68 – 69.

43. I.e., the coming of Jesus.

44. Is. 7:16.

45. Hebrew *musareha*, also, ethical teachings.

46. Matt. (not John) 5:39; cf. Lev. 19:18. An analysis of the Sermon on the Mount is given by David Flusser, *"Ha-'Torah' be-Derashah- ʿal- ha-Har,"* *Jewish Sources in Early Christianity*, Tel Aviv, 1979, pp. 226 – 234.

47. Cf. Deut. 29:17, and other verses.

48. Cf. Is. 49:7.

49. Lev. 19:18.

50. Lev. 19:17.

51. This is likely a reflection of the condition of Spanish Jewry after the persecutions of 1391, since the Jews felt helpless to defend themselves against Christian attacks.

52. I.e., Matt. 5 (the Sermon on the Mount).

53. Matt. 5:43 – 44; cf. Lev. 19:18.

54. Ps. 139:21.

55. This is a direct attack on Christian ethics. The Christian demands are so great that one cannot help but fail, since following one's natural inclination to anger, gluttony, or laziness leads to the loss of eternal life. This contention is directed against Paul, who had argued that the demands of the Torah are such that they lead necessarily to failure; see, for instance, Rom. 1 – 8. According to Thomas, from the aspect of its laws, the new religion is easier (*levior*) than the Torah of Moses, but from the aspect of internal actions, it is more difficult; see *Summa*, I – II, 107, 4. Duran, *Disgrace*, p. 55, called Christian ethics "foolish piety (*hasidiut shel shtut*)."

56. Hebrew *musareha*.

57. According to Thomas, the Ten Commandments are ethical laws of the Torah in comparison with the legal and ritual laws, and one may not change them; see *Summa*, I – II, 100, 3; 8. Thomas' division of the commandments was accepted by Duran (*Disgrace*, pp. 30 – 34); Shem Tov ibn Shaprut (*Even Bohan*, f. 11a); Simeon ben Zemah Duran (*Qeshet U-Magen*, Livorno, 1562/63 [reprinted, Jerusalem, 1969/70], pp. 12b – 13b); and Joseph Albo (*Sefer Ha-'Ikkarim*, III, 25). Crescas did not refer to this division at all.

58. E.g., Deut. 17:19; 28:58; 29:28; and other verses.

59. See Chapter 1, n. 30.

60. Cf. Matt. 5:18. see also Duran, *Disgrace*, pp. 24 – 29; *Epistle*, p. 80.

61. Lev. 11.

62. Lev. 18, 20.

63. Lev. 12 – 15.

64. Cf. Lev. 11:44, 45; 20:26.

65. Animality and pollution *(zohama')* are a result of original sin according to B. Avodah Zarah, 22b; Shabbat, 145b – 146a; Yevamot, 103b; see *Light of the Lord*, II, 2, 6, p. 38a – b; Lasker, "Original Sin."

66. Deut. 25:5 – 10.

67. Ex. 23:14 – 19; 34: 17 – 26; Lev. 23; Deut. 16.

68. Thomas, *SCG*, IV, 59.

69. See Thomas, *Summa*, I – II, 103, 3, ad 4. Thomas also said that the idea of a Sabbath is a moral principle, and, therefore, it is one of the Ten Commandments; it should still be observed. Nevertheless, the Sabbath Day itself is part of the ritual and one should not observe it *(Summa*, I – II, 110, 3, ad 2). See also II – II, 122, 4, ad 1.

70. I.e., the very day on which God ceased from labor during Creation, namely Saturday.

71. I.e., Sunday.

72. Deut. 29:28; cf. *Disgrace*, p. 28; *Epistle*, p. 79.

73. See *Guide*, II, 39; *Mishneh Torah*, "Foundations of the Torah," 9:1. It is possible that the words "And just as Maimonides, of blessed memory, said," are an addition by Joseph ben Shem Tov, since Crescas did not cite Maimonides in the entire *Refutation*.

74. Thomas, *Summa*, I – II, 98, 1; 98, 2, ad 4; 107, 2.

75. Gen. 5:24.

76. II Kings 2:3; Crescas used the examples of Enoch and Elijah in *Light of the Lord*, III, 3, 2, p. 81a.

77. The binding of Isaac (Gen. 22) was of central importance for Crescas; see *Light of the Lord*, II, 2, 6, p. 39a – b. According to Crescas, Israel has additional providence because of circumcision and the binding of Isaac.

78. See Chapters 1 – 2, and Lasker, "Original Sin."

79. Gen. 17:14. This verse was the basis of the Christian claim that circumcision was commanded as an atonement for original sin until the coming of Jesus. See V. Ermoni, "Circoncision," *Dictionnaire de théologie catholique*, vol. 2, Paris, 1910, p. 2525.

80. Crescas used this expression many times in *Light of the Lord*; see, e.g., pp. 16a, 26b, 73a. The meaning here is that if the Torah promises excision (*karet*) for those who do not observe the commandments, it is possible to conclude that it promises eternal life for those who do keep them.

81. Another example of understanding the position of the slaves in Egypt through reference to the Jewish experience in Spain.

82. See *Light of the Lord*, p. 74a. Saadia Gaon also mentioned the readiness of the patriarchs to die for their faith as a proof of the world to come; see *Beliefs and Opinions*, IX, 2. Moses Ha-Kohen of Tordesillas, who wrote his polemic *'Ezer Ha-'Emunah* twenty years before *The Refutation*, used a very similar argument; see Yehuda Shamir, *Rabbi Moses Ha-Kohen of Tordesillas and his Book 'Ezer Ha-Emunah — A Chapter in the History of the Judeo-Christian Controversy*, Coconut Grove, Fla., 1972, vol. 2, p. 27.

83. Num. 23:10.

84. Crescas used the example of Balaam in *Light of the Lord*, III, 2, 2, p. 71a.

85. One ms. adds Ps. 115:9.

86. Ps. 142:6.

87. Ps. 27:13.

88. Ps. 52:7.

89. See *Light of the Lord*, p. 37a.

90. Understanding *ḥayyim selah* in Ps. 52 as "life forever," according to B. Eruvin, 54a; see also Maimonides, *Mishneh Torah,* "Laws of Repentance," 8, 6.

91. I Sam. 22:17 – 19; according to M. Sanhedrin, 10, 2, Doeg has no portion in the world to come. This section of *The Refutation* has been discussed recently by Warren (Zeev) Harvey, "R. Hasdai Crescas and Bernat Netge on the Soul," *Jerusalem Studies in Jewish Thought,* 5 (1985/86): 149, n. 37 (in Hebrew).

92. This passage apparently was written by Joseph ben Shem Tov even though there is no such indication of it in any of the manuscripts. The reference to "the knowledge of opposites is one" indicates the authorship of the translator.

93. Ps. 52:8; this is the continuation of the last verse cited by Crescas earlier.

94. Is. 45:17.

95. Cf. Ex. 19:5 – 6.

96. Deut. 33:29.

97. Cf. Ps. 107:10, and other verses.

98. *The Book of Yossipon,* ed., David Flusser, vol. 1, Jerusalem, 1978/79; vol. 2, Jerusalem, 1980/81. See also *Light of the Lord,* p. 82a.

99. Cf. Maimonides, *Guide,* III, 32.

100. Ex. 15:26.

101. Cf. *Light of the Lord* 3:3:1, p. 72a.

102. Cf. Maimonides, *Commentary on the Mishnah,* "Introduction to Chapter Ḥeleq."

103. Prov. 16:15.

104. I Kings 5:18.

105. Cf. Maimonides, "Introduction to Chapter Ḥeleq"; *Mishneh Torah,* "Laws of Kings," 12, 5; on the basis of Is. 11:9. See also *Guide,* III, 11.

106. Cf. Deut. 11:22.

CHAPTER 10
CONCERNING DEMONS

1. In Crescas' Preface, it is stated that the angels sinned with pride and jealously; see Thomas, *Summa*, I, 63, 2.

2. For the Christian belief, see Epistle of John 1:3, 8; Thomas, *Summa*, I, 63 – 64; *SCG*, III, 108 – 110; Fourth Lateran Council, in *Denz.*, no. 428. Crescas mentioned the Christian belief in *Light of the Lord*, IV, 6, p. 89b.

3. According to some Christians, the sin was not actually in the very first instant of existence; see Thomas, *Summa*, I, 62; Albertus Magnus, *Commentarii in II Sententiarum*, Dist. III, Art. 14 in *Opera Omnia*, vol. 27, Paris, 1894, pp. 87 – 88; Duns Scotus, *Quaestiones in Secundum Librum Sententiarum*, Dist. V, Quaest. II, in *Opera Omnia*, vol. 12, Paris, 1893, p. 315. Yet Bonaventura did hold the opinion that the sin was actually in the very first instant; see *Commentaire des Sentences*, in *Opera*, Lyon, 1688, In IV Sent. 1, II, dist. III, part II, a. 1, q. 1, 2.

4. I.e., contradicting the Christian claim that the demons were originally good angels who willfully sinned.

5. Aristotle, *Physics*, IV, 11, 219b, 19 – 220a, 25; the reference here to Book I is most likely an error, though that reading is attested in the manuscripts.

6. For Crescas' theory of free will and determinism, see *Light of the Lord*, II, 5, pp. 45b – 50b; Aviezer Ravitzky, "Crescas' Theory on Human Will: Development and Sources," *Tarbiz*, 51 (1981/82): 445 – 469 (in Hebrew); Seymour Feldman, "Crescas' Theological Determinism," *Daat*, 9 (Summer 1982): 3 – 28; *idem*, "A Debate Concerning Determinism in Late Medieval Jewish Philosophy," *Proceedings of the American Academy for Jewish Research*, 51 (1984): 15 – 54; Warren (Zeev) Harvey, "The Expression 'Feeling of Compulsion' in Crescas," *Jerusalem Studies in Jewish Thought*, 4:3 – 4 (1984/85): pp. 275 – 280 (in Hebrew).

7. It has already been pointed out in Chapter 3 that time does not consist of continuous, discrete instants of time.

8. Aristotle, *Physics*, VI, 4; see also Chapter 3, n. 12; Chapter 6, nn. 11 – 13.

9. All the manuscripts read, "did not remain."

10. On the free will of demons, see Thomas, *Summa*, I, 64, 2.
Crescas' argument is as follows: if the angels were punished and free will was removed from them, this occurred on one of two possible opportunities: (1) immediately at the time of the sin; or (2) after the sin. If they were punished after the sin (2), then this was (a) some time after they had sinned during which they still had free will; or (b) in the instant immediately after the instant of the sin. But since time is not composed of instants, the punishment could not have started the instant immediately after the instant of the sin (b). Therefore, if the angels were punished after they sinned (2), for some time after the sin they retained their free will (a). The Christians were not willing to believe that the angels existed for some time after the sin with their free will; they stated that the angels were punished immediately with the sin (1). If that were so, Crescas argued, in the same first instant of existence, the angels had free will (with which they sinned), and they did not have free will (as a result of their punishment).

11. Thomas, *Summa*, I, 62.

12. This is a Neo-Platonic theory and is not in Aristotle's *Metaphysics*. Crescas perhaps took it from one of Aristotle's commentators.

13. Cf. *Guide* II, 7; see also II, 6; I, 49.

14. The argument is as follows: if the demons were good angels who did, indeed, have free will enabling them to sin, they must have used that free will purposefully; yet the purposeful use of free will presumes that the will preceded the actions; therefore, the demons must have existed as good angels for some time before they sinned, a conclusion which the Christians did not accept.

15. Deut. 32:17.

16. Lev. 17:7.

17. Matt. 4:1 – 11; Mark 1:12 – 13; Luke 4:1 – 13.

18. Matt. 8:28 – 34; Mark 1:23 – 27; 9:14 – 29; Luke 8:32 – 39.

19. IV, 6; p. 89a – b; Crescas agreed that (1) demons exist, and (2) that nothing evil can come from God.

20. See Alexander Altmann, "Gersonides' Commentary on Averroes' Epitome of *Parva Naturalia*, II.3: Annotated Critical Edition," *Proceedings of the American Academy for Jewish Research*, Jubilee Volume, 46 – 47 (1978 – 79): 10, n. 15.

21. Deut. 32:17.

22. Sifre to Deut. 32:17.

23. *Guide*, III, 46.

24. *Ibid.*, I, 7; III, 22, 46.

25. See, e.g., B. Berakhot, 6a; Pesaḥim, 112b; Yoma, 75a; and many other places in Rabbinic works. See also Urbach, *The Sages*, pp. 161 – 165.

26. See n. 19.

27. *Guide*, III, 10 – 12.

28. I.e., that God causes no essential evil.

29. Hebrew *mazziqim*.

30. See Isaiah Tishby, *Mishnat Ha-Zohar*, I, 3d ed., Jerusalem, 1970/71, pp. 361 – 377.

31. See Chapter 4, n. 37.

32. These terms refer to the different meanings of language. Univocal words are used with one meaning; equivocal words are used with totally different meanings; amphibolous words are used with some sort of common meaning; see *Guide*, introduction; I, 56.

33. Some manuscripts read, "will not find."

34. Literally, those who have a tradition.

35. Sifre to Deut. 17:11; *Light of the Lord*, III, 5, 2, p. 78b.

36. Hebrew "ve-'im qabbala neqabbeil be-seiver panim yafot"; Crescas used the same expression in *Light of the Lord* in reference to reincarnation, IV, 7, p. 89b; see Harvey, "Elements," pp. 102 – 103. On the relationship between Joseph ben Shem Tov and Kabbalah, see Regev, *Joseph*, pp. 241 – 251.

37. According to Joseph ben Shem Tov, it is hard for a philosopher to explain the existence and essence of demons. Nevertheless, since there is a Jewish religious tradition that demons exist, it must be possible to provide solutions to the philosophical problems, but this is not the place to do so.

38. Cf. Prov. 22:21.

39. Hence, similar to Duran, Crescas wrote two polemical works, one using exegetical arguments, which is lost, and one using philosophical arguments (the present work).

40. *Commentary on the Epistle*, p. 22; Lasker, *Polemics*, pp. 13 – 16.

41. See Regev, *Joseph*, pp. 7 – 9.

42. A city in Castile.

43. August, 1451. Concerning the speed of Joseph's work, see the Foreword to the English Translation.

44. From the *'Amidah* prayer on the High Holidays.

45. Is. 11:9; see also the end of Joseph ben Shem Tov's Introduction and the end of Chapter 9.

46. Joseph ben Shem Tov used a similar ending in his *Commentary on the Epistle*; see p. 152 (and in manuscripts of the *Commentary on the Epistle*, the similarity is even greater).

SELECT BIBLIOGRAPHY

Abravanel, Isaac, *Shamayim Hadashim*, Roedelheim, 1828 (reprinted, Jerusalem, 1966/67).

Baer, Yitzhaq (Fritz), *A History of the Jews in Christian Spain*, Philadelphia, 1971.

Berger, David, *The Jewish-Christian Debate in the High Middle Ages*, Philadelphia, 1979.

Bergh, Simon van den, *Averroes' Tahafut Al-Tahafut (The Incoherence of the Incoherence)*, London, 1954.

Bland, Kalman, ed., *The Epistle on the Possibility of Conjunction with the Active Intellect by Ibn Rushd with the Commentary of Moses Narboni*, New York, 1982.

Bouyges, Maurice, ed., *Algazel Tahafot Al-Falasifat*, Beirut, 1927.

————. ed., *Averroes Tafsir Ma Ba'd At-Tabi'at*, Beirut, 1948.

————. ed., *Tahafot al-Tahafot*, Beirut, 1930.

Crescas, Hasdai, *Or Adonai (Light of the Lord)*, Vienna, 1859 (reprinted, n.p., n.d.).

Denziger, Henrici, *Enchiridion Symbolorum* (different editions).

De Rossi, Joh. Bern., *Bibliotheca Judaica Anti-Christiana*, Parma, 1800 (reprinted, Amsterdam, 1969).

Duran, Profiat, *Iggeret Al Tehi Ka-'Avotekha (Epistle Be Not Like Your Fathers)*, in Talmage, *Polemical Writings*.

————. *Sefer Kelimmat Ha-Goyim (The Disgrace of the Gentiles)*, in *ibid.*

Feldman, Seymour, "The Theory of Eternal Creation in Hasdai Crescas and Some of his Predecessors," *Viator*, 11(1980): 289 – 320.

Harvey, Warren (Zeev), "Crescas versus Maimonides on Knowledge and Pleasure," in Ruth-Link Salinger, ed., *A Straight Path. Studies in Medieval Philosophy and Culture. Essays in Honor of Arthur Hyman*, Washington, D.C., 1988, pp. 113 – 123.

————. *Hasdai Crescas's Critique of the Theory of the Acquired Intellect*, Columbia University dissertation, 1973.

————. "Kabbalistic Elements in Crescas' Light of the Lord," *Jerusalem Studies in Jewish Thought*, II:1 (1982/83): 101 – 103 (in Hebrew).

————. "The Term *Hitdabbekut* in Crescas' Definition of Time," *Jewish Quarterly Review*, 71:1 (1980-81): 44 – 47.

Joseph ben Shem Tov, *Commentary on the Epistle Be Not Like Your Fathers*, in the edition of Duran's *Epistle*, published by the Akademon, Hebrew University, Jerusalem, 1969/70, on the basis of the Adolf (Zev) Poznanski manuscript, Jewish National and University Library ms. Heb 8° 757.

————. *Sefer Kevod Elohim (The Glory of God)*, Ferrara, 1555 (reprinted, n.p., n.d.).

Kamali, Sabih A., *Al-Ghazali's Tahafut Al-Falasifah*, Lahore, 1958.

Kellner, Menachem, *Dogma in Medieval Jewish Thought*, Oxford, 1986.

Lasker, Daniel J., "Averroistic Trends in Jewish-Christian Polemics in the Late Middle Ages," *Speculum*, 55:2 (1980): 294 – 304.

————. *Hasdai Crescas' Bittul Iqqarei Ha-Noẓrim*, Ramat-Gan and Beer Sheva, 1990.

————. *Jewish Philosophical Polemics Against Christianity in the Middle Ages*, New York, 1977.

————. "Original Sin and its Atonement According to Ḥasdai Crescas," *Daat*, 20 (Winter, 1988): 127 – 135 (in Hebrew).

————. "Transubstantiation, Elijah's Chair, Plato, and the Jewish-Christian Debate," *Revue des Études Juives*, 143:1 – 2 (Jan. – June, 1984): 31 – 58.

Levi ben Gershom, *Sefer Milḥamot Adonai (Wars of the Lord)*, Riva di Trento, 1560 (reprinted, n.p., n.d.).

Migne, Jacques P., ed., *Patrologiae Cursus Completus. . . Series Latina [PL]*, 221 vols., Paris, 1844 – 66.

Moses ben Maimon (Maimonides), *Guide of the Perplexed*.

Moses ben Nahman, *Disputation of Barcelona*, in Ch. D. Chavel, ed., *Kitvei Rabbeinu Moshe ben Nahman*, Vol. I, Jerusalem, 1962/63, pp. 297 – 320 (in Hebrew).

Netanyahu, Ben-Zion, *The Marranos of Spain*, New York, 1966.

Pines, Shlomo, "Scholasticism after Thomas Aquinas and the Teachings of Hasdai Crescas and his Predecessors," *Proceedings of the Israel Academy of Sciences and Humanities*, I, 10, Jerusalem, 1967.

Ravitsky, Aviezer, *Crescas' Sermon on the Passover and Studies in his Philosophy*, Jerusalem, 1988 (in Hebrew).

————. "Crescas' Theory on Human Will: Development and Sources," *Tarbiz*, 51 (1981/82): 445 – 469 (in Hebrew).

Regev, Shaul, *Theology and Rational Mysticism in the Writings of R. Joseph ben Shem Tov*, Hebrew University dissertation, June, 1983 (in Hebrew).

Rosenberg, Shalom, "The *Arba'ah Turim* of Rabbi Abraham bar Judah, Disciple of Don Hasdai Crescas," *Jerusalem Studies in Jewish Thought*, 3:4 (1983/84): 525 – 621 (in Hebrew).

Talmage, Frank, *The Polemical Writings of Profiat Duran*, Jerusalem, 1981 (in Hebrew).

Thomas Aquinas, *Summa Contra Gentiles.*

———. *Summa Theologiae.*

Urbach, Ephraim E., *The Sages — Their Concepts and Beliefs*, Jerusalem, 1975.

Wolfson, Harry A., *Crescas' Critique of Aristotle*, Cambridge, Mass., 1929.

———. "Extradeical and Intradeical Interpretations of Platonic Ideas," *Religious Philosophy*, New York, 1965, pp. 27 – 68.

———. *The Philosophy of Spinoza*, Cambridge, Mass., 1961.

———. *The Philosophy of the Church Fathers*, Vol. 1, Cambridge, Mass., 1964.

———. *The Philosophy of the Kalam*, Cambridge, Mass., and London, 1976.

———. *Studies in the History of Philosophy and Religion*, vol. 1, Cambridge, Mass, 1973; vol. 2, Cambridge, Mass., and London, 1978.

INDEX OF SOURCES

Rabbinic Literature

Aristotle

Jewish Sources

Bonaventure
Commentary on Sententiae   IV, Dist. 11, 1   118
IV, 1, 11, Dist. III,
Part II, a.1, q. 1, 2   130

Dons Scotus
Quaestiones in Secundum Librum Sententiarum   Dist. v, Q. II   130

Hugo de Saint Victor
Summa Sententiarum   VI, 4   119

Innocent III
De Sacro Altaris Mysterio   IV, 12   116

John of Salisbury
Historia Pontificalis   8   109

Lombard, Peter
Sententiae   I, 8, 9   109
I, 10   110
IV, Dist. 12, 1   119

Nicolas of Cusa
Of Learned Ignorance   108

Ockham, William
De Corpore Christi   119

Peter Alphonsus
Dialogus   X   101

Ratramnus
De Eo Quod Christus ex Virgine Natus Est   117

Thomas Aquinas
Commentary on Sententiae   I, 10   110
De Potentia   9, 9   110
Summa Contra Gentiles   I, 7   96
I, 28   103
I, 42   103
II, 25   96
III, 108–110   130
IV, 10   102, 109
IV, 14   102, 109
IV, 16   103

GENERAL INDEX

155